# DREAMS,
## REVELATIONS,
## AND
## MANIFESTATIONS

PHYLLIS BAKER

iUniverse®

# DREAMS, REVELATIONS, AND MANIFESTATIONS

*Scripture taken from the New King James Version®. Copyright © 1982 by Thomas Nelson. Used by permission. All rights reserved.*

*iUniverse books may be ordered through booksellers or by contacting:*

*iUniverse*
*1663 Liberty Drive*
*Bloomington, IN 47403*
*www.iuniverse.com*
*844-349-9409*

*ISBN: 978-1-6632-4014-9 (sc)*
*ISBN: 978-1-6632-4116-0 (e)*

*Library of Congress Control Number: 2022911148*

*Print information available on the last page.*

*iUniverse rev. date: 10/21/2022*

"The Universe has information, and we are connected to that information through, Dreams, Revelations, and Manifestations"
Dr. Phyllis Baker

# Contents

# Acknowledgements

I would like to take this opportunity to acknowledge and thank my family, Zenovious Stripling and Abner Stripling (Parents, deceased) Robert Baker Junior & Senior, Brian Baker, Riyah Baker, Raquel Baker and Brian Baker Jr. Vanessa Baker and Jessica Martinez, for their support and love.

I would also like to express my appreciation to my former students/scholars/supporters, Bianca Metayer, Luke Nelson, and Sophia Michelle Humel for assisting me with the manuscript.

All my friends and former students that listen to me, and shared their dreams. And of course, the Creator/God for giving me this gift, and all gifts.

# Dreams

Dreams are your sanctuary of understanding, your sanctuary of creativity, your sanctuary of rest, your sanctuary of correction, your sanctuary of adventure, and your sanctuary of spiritual connectivity and awareness. Dreams are avenues of revelations, and possibly manifestations. Are you ready for a great adventure! This is an opportunity for the spectacular to unfold and where an opportunity to take a journey through your own mind is possible! In the words of Carl Jung as he wrote relating to dreams: "Prepare to be confronted." Dreams matter! Anthropologists tell us that one of the primary reasons why religion was started is because humans since time and memorial have had prophetic dreams. Dreams that have manifested, dreams that provided direction, dreams that have led to insight, dreams of communicating with departed loved ones, dreams that have come true! With this level of experimental knowledge, there was no doubt or hesitancy to believe in a God-force, in an intelligence, and power that was superior to their own.

## What are dreams?

According to Carl Jung, dreams are a normal psychic phenomenon that transmits unconscious reactions or spontaneous impulses to the consciousness.

According to Rabbi Yehuda Berg, Dreams are the technology of the soul. An opportunity to connect to our source, a private instrument, and a "Navigation system".

The soul is connected to its source each night. Our main problem as human beings is that we focus our attention in the wrong place. Wouldn't it be nice to get periodic communication from God? We do, and they are called dreams. This is our inheritance, our birthright, and our potential. We are custodians of light. (Berg)

**Dreams are agents of the spirit**
**A dimension of Mind**
**A communication device**
**Guides**

Dreams are a metaphysical experience that occurs while sleeping, where images, sounds, ideas and events are occurring. (Baker) For some dreams are viewed as a way of rebooting the brain, getting rid of mental clutter and internal conflicts. For me, dreams are a communication device; a way that the Higher Self/ God the Creator, communes with us. A transmission of information.

What is a Dream? "A dream is an event perceived by the brain during the REM phase of normal sleep" (Innes, 2000)

Dreams want our attention; they are messages that must be communicated. Dreams can show up as a direct message or can be expressed in symbolic language. "Ever since Sigmund Freud, MD, demonstrated in his seminal 1899 work, The Interpretation of Dreams, that dreams are psychologically noteworthy events with inherent meaning, the ideas of dreams carrying messages has grown in the West. If a dream does have something important to tell us about our life, our relationship, or our health, it will highly be likely, repeated even if someone wakes us up in the middle of it, or if we forget it upon waking, or if we become lucid and decide not to stay with it. Dream messages repeating themselves can be clearly seen with recurrent nightmares, or a series of bad dreams that turn around the same theme. If the lucid dreamer decides to fly away from a dream monster or wake herself up, she is effectively making a date to meet that same dream situation again another night. Our dreaming mind will not stop trying to bring emotional conflicts to our attention until we have faced them.

Why a second book on dreams? Because the topic is just that important, and the revelations have not been exhausted. Why focus on dreams? I believe that dreams can be an essential starting point and a constant, to one's spiritual exploration and growth. I think that the ability to dream has been given to us as a communication devise, and an Antenor of sort, given to us by our creator to help us navigate our lives. I would also like to suggest that dreams are a central and primary way for one to examine their psycho-spiritual world.

I hold that G-d will reveal secrets and messages to you through the process of dreaming, so that the value of dreams cannot be overstated. Speak Lord, Speak, for we need your guidance and help...so that we may live and not die, so we can live our best lives, improve our health, define our relationships, help our friends and family. For how can we pray for things that we are not aware of?

The Dream State has served us since recorded history in a number of ways, by providing:

> Prophetic Dreams
> Informational Dreams
> Directional Dreams
> Guidance
> Purification Dreams
> Beauty during the dreaming process
> Instructional Dreams
> Healing Dreams
> Multi- Plane Communication Dreams

Why should we be concerned about dreams? The answer is that Dreams are important. Dreams have fascinated humanity since time and memorial. It is something that all cultures do, regardless of race, religion, or philosophy, and belief. For this reason alone, this universal principle is worthy of our investigation. I believe that in every culture, there are individuals that have had or have known someone who has had a precognitive or psychic dream that has come true.

*Phyllis Baker*

Understanding our dreams, and the dreaming process, is a way to help us understand ourselves in a deeper and more meaningful way. A method of integration, self-awareness, synthesis and self-actualization, awaits us that is so profound, and extraordinary; one should take the time and create a space for dream understanding.

# The Science of Sleep and Dreaming

It is believed that sleep and dreaming happens in cycles or stages:

1. The hypnagogic state, where the body relaxes and prepares for sleep. This stage is characterized by a sensation of floating or drifting often accompanied by a jumble of images, voices or landscapes that are vague or shifts in colors.
2. The initial stage. The eyes are closed, the brain is still awake, but one feels sleepy. The Alpha Waves (responsible for relaxation) which also can enhance creativity and inspiration are present.
3. True Sleep. The brain is now generating Theta Brainwaves.
4. Deep Sleep Stage is characterized by Delta Brainwaves. At this stage waking is very difficult, and if awaken, there is an intense desire to go back to sleep.

5. Dreaming. Characterized by Rapid Eye Movement (REM), this stage lasts about ten minutes initially, increasing to about an hour towards the end of the night's sleep.

After stage five, the brain returns to stage two and the cycle starts over again. It is believed that each cycle lasts around 90 minutes, so in eight-hour night's sleep the average person will have at least four dreams and sometimes many more. (Taylor p.8)

I.  Sleep and dreaming are two of the most important aspects of life, yet we know so little about what happens when we do. Sleep helps to enrich many essential functions such as:

(A) The ability to learn
(B) Memorize
(C) Make logical choices and decisions
(D) Recalibrates our emotional brain circuits
(E) Improves our immune system
(F) Helps fight infection and malignancies
(G) Refines the metabolic state by balancing our insulin and glucose levels
(H) Regulates our appetite, and controls body weight
(I) Maintains microbiomes within the gut
(J) Sleep is connected to the health of our cardiovascular system, and helps in lowering blood pressure
(K) It helps to reset our brain and body health

II. Sleep is the 3rd most important factor in good health, the other two are:

(A) Diet
(B) Exercise

III. Lack of sleep affect every cell in your body

IV. The leading cause of death and disease

"Little sleep, short life span"

(A) Heart disease
(B) Obesity
(C) Dementia
(D) Diabetes
(E) Cancer

All of the above have a causal links to a lack of sleep.
(Walker, M. "Why we Sleep)

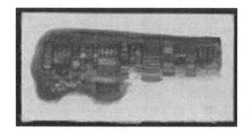

## About this Item

**Title**

[Gilgamesh dreaming] / Bernarda Bryson.

**Summary**

Drawing for book illustration shows Gilgamesh sleeping in a room with colorful columns.

**Contributor Names**

Bryson, Bernarda, artist

**Created / Published**

[Roosevelt, New Jersey], [ca. 1966]

**Subject Headings**

- Gilgamesh–(Legendary character)
- Gilgamesh–Adaptations
- Sleeping
- Columns

**Headings**

Book illustrations–1960-1970.
Watercolors–1960-1970.

## Notes

- Title from item.
- Gift; The Bernarda Bryson Shahn Family, LLC; 2012; (DLC/PP-2012:052).
- Published in: Gilgamesh; man's first story, written and illustrated by Bernarda Bryson. New York: Holt, Rinehart & Winston, [1967].
- Accession box no. DLC/PP-2012:052

## Medium

1 drawing: watercolor and ink; sheet 27 x 51 cm.

## Call Number/Physical Location

Unprocessed in PR 13 CN 2012:052 [item] [P&P]

## Repository

Library of Congress Prints and Photographs Division Washington, D.C. 20540 USA http://hdl.loc.gov/loc.pnp/pp.print

# Types of Dreams

## Precognitive Dreams

Precognitive Dreams are often called sixth sense dreams or psychic dreams. These dreams foretell the future. These dreams have even saved lives, by avoiding some action or event. These dreams also serve as a warning and allow for preparation, or one may engage in prayer to prevent, or delay an event.

## Lucid Dreams

Lucid Dreams are those in which the dreamer is aware that he or she is dreaming. The dreams are vivid and clear, and one may even be able to take control or direct the dream in a given direction. These dreams are rare, but there are steps that you can take to help you become a more lucid dreamer. Record on a piece of paper this statement "Tonight I will have a lucid dream."

## Surreal Dreams

Surreal Dreams are often otherworldly dreams. They may be complex and difficult to understand. Images and landscapes are often distorted. Surreal Dreams can be stimulated by extraordinary encounters, a book, play, movie, foreign travel, etc.

Surreal Dreams have their own logic, which may have little relationship to the waking world. It is like looking through fog, floating, in a maze, or even shifting in time and space. When you engage a dream of this nature, strip away as much as possible the strangeness and look for the basics.

## Nightmares

Many nightmares start out as ordinary dreams, later turning dark and scary. The helplessness you feel in this dream is the worst. It is generally how you feel about a fear in your waking life. Occasionally, a nightmare is your subconscious punishing you for something you have or have not done. Sometimes a nightmare is a strong negative feeling you have against the person, situation, or thing in question. It may also be a fear you have about someone you are very close to or you, yourself. (Young)

# Communicating with your Dreams
## "I and the father are one"

Dreams, like death, hypnosis, trance, and alternative forms of unconsciousness or semi unconsciousness are what I believe to be are another dimension of existence. This is why I believe we can communicated with God, the deceased, obtain new ideas, creativity, be healed and receive revelations in our dreams. In a real sense, you must in some degree cross over. My grandmother came to me all upset. She was intense in her facial expressions and her body movements, which indicated to me that she was upset with me. She was surrounded by a group of others, I assume were other loved ones, but I could not discern who they were. Being the matriarch of the family she was the spokesperson. She spoke in a language I did not understand, but she informed me there was something she wanted me to do, and that was to love and care for my relatives. As she left me in the dream, her face was transformed to Debra (my cousin), who is the daughter of my uncle and one of my grandmother's beloved grandchildren.

When I awoke I pondered the meaning of this dream, what did grandmother want me to do? I thought it had something to do with the fact that at the last family reunion I promised to submit a proposal to host the next reunion in Miami. More especially on Miami Beach. I immediately got on the project, got the hotel arrangements, made an agenda and submitted the proposal. This is not all that grandmother wanted me to do.

My sister called and informed me that my aunt, Debra, and Clarice's mother had made her transition. I knew she was not well and even knew she was going into hospice, but I failed to call or visit my cousin Clarice who only lives around 40 miles away, I thought I would do if I had more time. I am so ashamed and disappointed. As I spoke with my cousin Clarice, (who in earlier times we were, much closer and supported each other, both living in South Florida, our parents are from Georgia) I recounted the dream with grandmother a few weeks prior, and she said that grandmother was trying to tell you that "**we are family**".

I want to do better! I had not experienced my grandmother in a dream in over twenty years, so this was significant. I want to do better with these messages. I want to seize the moments that are available, and I want to do the right thing. Prior to this event happening, I wanted to write a book that dealt with communicating with dreams. Now in retrospect, I should have asked grandmother, what you would like me to do as opposed to try to decode the message on my own. She was right there, I should have asked. In working with our dreams, we must break through the barrier of fear and communicate more. An ongoing dialogue should be established in the dream and continue when we awake.

Most people believe that you are in the twilight zone when you are dreaming. I believe that you are the twilight zone when you do not access the meaning of your dreams. Whereby the can be used for integration and wholeness. In this sense you are truly alive and functional at all levels.

I am taking the position of Charles Fillmore who stated "If this God you say exist, and really exist, we must be able in some way, to communicate".

Anthropologists tell us that humans have had the ability to speak for about 150,000 years. According to scientists it is because a muted gene, FOXP2 had been turned on. In the case of other primates this gene is still muted, and they are unable to speak. Do we have a muted gene that can be turned on to communicate with our dreams? If language is transmitted through learning, Can learning to communicate in our dreams also be learned? Can we learn our specific dream signs and dream symbols? Or is it possible to speak to and hear from our dreams directly?

Linguistic Anthropology is interesting in features of language that compare, variate, and change. Can we apply this science to our dreams?

I think we can but it will require study, time, desire and will; and what I feel is most important is the application of spiritual disciplines. In a real sense, I am asking you to become a Dream Linguistic Anthropologist. We can, however, borrow for this discipline that is already established. Unfortunately, there is no school or university course offered in this discipline, you must call on the master teacher to assist you. I have been inspired to write this book, and I believe I can help, along with other inspired teachers and books, and your own divine revelations.

Speech reflects social differences like dream communication reflects a different level of intricate integration of memory, spiritual attunement, clarity in thought, and the power of imagination. You must think in your dreams, you must remember the dream and you must remember that you are dreaming, and speak up in the dream.

Ask questions, say no, (the power of denial) if there is something that you don't want to do or want to happen. Agree (The Power of affirmations) with the dream if you do.

A basic level of language is the "call system," other primates use this system. Calling is a noncomplex form of communication using various tones and sounds in varying forms of intensity. Try to speak in your dreams or use the call system. This will help you to communicate until you can develop your ability to speak. Follow the evolutionary chain to develop your dream language. Sound is a basic form of language and communication. That is why music, chanting, and various vocalizations can be transformative. There is something registering on a subconscious or super conscious level, or spiritual level. Try humming or singing or listening to music before bed and see if there is a carryover effect in your dreams.

Another developmental level in language is sign language. Different animals are able to learn sign language. I am proposing that we too can use sign language until we are able to speak or hear in our dreams. But remember this can be limiting as in the case of my grandmother's communication to me, she was ahead of me. She was moving so fast and with such intensity, I did not get it, or maybe I was caught off guard. This brings up another point, preparation. You must be ready, and stay ready. Think about it, if primates can sustain a family life, negotiate food, compromise, and life itself, calling and sign language must be very effective and significant.

Humans, like other primates can study sign language, can use productivity. Productivity is defined as "Creating new expressions that are comprehensible to the other speaker." (Kottar, 2011, p.314) In our dream life, we should be mindful that we have this ability. I am asking you to become more active and proactive in your dream life and observe your development, growth, and your evolution in the realm of communication. This is done through programming and training. If apes and monkeys can be trained to communicate. (primarily using repetition and applied learning) in ways in which they can understand each other, can't we too find a way to break the code to our own communication with the cosmic mind, ourselves?

Language is symbolic communication. It allows for information to be stored, we can understand things we have not experienced, transmit information about us to others, anticipate responses, a vehicle for learning, and is adaptive. (Kottar) What about dream language? It can offer us even more, because this language is originating in a domain that is not human or limited by human experiences.

# Mysticism

People all over the world have claimed to have mystical encounters and experiences. Mysticism is concerned with the possibility of personally encountering a spiritual reality that is hidden from our normal awareness. A Mystic is a person who seeks direct knowledge of Ultimate Reality through the power of thought, ritual, and contemplation. The Mystics teach us that higher consciousness is available to everyone regardless of race, religion, culture, or creed. The purpose of this chapter is to examine the basic ideas and practices of various societies and attempt to identify the universal principles, ideas, and methods inherent in them. Additionally the focus of this book is to identify the principles (how something works or the overall plan) of mysticism.

"Mysticism begins with the extraordinary experiences of the ancient shamans of primal peoples who, through the use of ritual and psychedelic plants, began an exploration of the mysteries of consciousness. In India, this wisdom flowered into a profound philosophy which gradually influenced the whole of the ancient world. Ancient Egypt, which gave birth to the Mystery Schools—spiritual universities for mystical initiation. The philosophy of India and Egypt came together in ancient Greece. Here, the Mystery school flourished as a religion (school of thought) for a thousand years, and left a legacy that would inspire the Western World. The original purpose and function of every faith, every mythology, and every philosophical system has been integration, what Carl Jung called 'individuation.' This process entails personal evolution and psychic growth centered on the emerging self." (Sargent, 1994, p. xxiii) The goal of individuation is to help one find their psychic balance and center. This centering or coming home to self can lead to wholeness, self-actualization, and self-realization, and yes, self-integration.

The relationship of mysticism to religion has been characterized by a cycle of living revelation bringing life to dead traditions, only to fall in turn into religious orthodoxy. In sixth-century BC India, the Buddha experienced enlightenment and challenged the authorities of the Hindu religion, becoming the founder of a new mystical faith.

Each mystical tradition has gone through different high points and low points. Jewish mysticism reached its heights with the Kabbalist of the middle Ages, and the Hasid of the eighteenth century. Christian Mysticism was most vibrant among the Gnostic of the first century AD and the "Friends of God" of the thirteenth and fourteenth centuries. Islamic mysticism flowered with the Sufis of the tenth to twelfth centuries. All traditions have had their great saints and sages, who directly experienced the eternal truth and left a legacy of spiritual inspirations for those who followed.

In the modern world, there is growing disillusionment with orthodox dogmatic religion and scientific materialism that cannot satisfy the longing of the soul. This has indeed led to a spiritual hunger. The Mystics offer us their personal testimonies that this hunger can be satisfied through a direct experience with mystical dimensions of life. This vision may be glimpsed through the window of any one of their accounts of rapture and their inspired insights.

There are mystics that have flourished outside of any religious tradition, like the scientists who received their insight from angels. The array of great masters and different spiritual paths is only an outer veil covering the essential simplicity of the mystic's message. This mystical journey will assist us in discovering, in the daily unfolding of our lives, something so obvious it was overlooked: the Mystery of life.

"Mystics do not have to produce documents as evidence of their direct experiences of ultimate reality. Nonetheless, most mystics who become knowledgeable and exert significant influence on others do produce documents." (Carmody & Carmody, p. 238)

"Mystics want to meet, deal with, praise, and be transformed by the best, the brightest, the most ultimate reality there is." (Carmody & Carmody, p. 298)

"The mentality at work here is artistic, symbolic, mythic, archetypal, and participative— gather whatever other adjectives seem good." (Carmody & Carmody, p. 285)

Although the mystics are forced to use words to communicate, they really want to bring our attention to the silence within which words are not spoken. Mystical knowledge is like knowing a country because you have been there. It is not a collection of facts to be studied. It is a state of knowing. It is immediate and alive. It is natural and open to all of us, no matter our level of education or intellectual sophistication. Jesus was the son of a carpenter, the mystical poet Kabir was a weaver, and the guru Sri Nisargadatta was practically illiterate; yet like all such masters, their teachings show a depth of understanding and astuteness of mind that comes from a firsthand experience of the nature of reality.

Mystical knowing is an overwhelming and blissful experience of love and rapture. The mystics look with their hearts and find the heart of the ultimate entity—an all-encompassing compassion that needs not intellectual justification. Mystics of all traditions confront our most basic assumption about ourselves and the lives we lead. They speak as individual people, yet they talk of not being confined by a physical body, or even having a separate personal identity at all.

Mysticism offers a radical, and individual solution to the trials and tribulations of life. It also offers the possibility of a new life in a new world, simply by transforming our awareness. The great mystics are the explorers of this new world we are now envisioning by questioning our common sense beliefs and by stretching our imaginations.

Mysticism is not a religion; it is not concerned with beliefs and doctrines, but a methodology used by people all over the world. Mysticism is a contemplation of the essential mysteries of life. It confronts the questions that many ask, 'Who am I?' and 'What is the purpose of life?' The mystics do not want to have blind faith in particular religious creeds, but rather to set out on a personal exploration of consciousness. They are open to new possibilities, willing to be surprised, to have their world turned upside down, to let go of the safety of mass consciousness and embark on their own spiritual journey to find their own intuitive sense of meaning. This is why they have so often been labeled as heretics and non-conformists. Alchemy is a branch of Mysticism. "Certainly we can date the principles of alchemy back in time to the ancient Egyptians, for whom it was the master science. The Chaldeans, Phoenicians, and Babylonians were also familiar with the principles of alchemy, as were many people of the orient. It was practiced in ancient Greece, and Rome. During the middle ages it was a science, a religion as well as a philosophy. Often seen as rebels against the religion of their day, alchemists would hide their philosophical teachings under the allegory of gold-making. In this manner they were able to continue their art and ways, receiving only ridicule rather than persecution and death." (Wolf, p. 3)

Chemistry evolved from alchemy, however the two schools had very little in common. Chemistry has to do with verifiable science, while alchemy explores the hidden and higher levels of reality. This reality is the foundation of all spirituality. "Some commentators claim alchemy to be wholly a spiritual discipline, while others seem interested only in finding out when gold was actually made and by whom: Both attitudes are misleading. It is essential to keep in mind that there are precise correspondences, fundamental to alchemical thought, between the visible and the invisible, above and below, matter and spirit, plants and metals." (Wolf, p. 4)

Alchemy is a transmutative process! It is the process of understanding various universal and symbolic codes and allowing these codes to become alive within the individual to connect him or her to a higher reality.

In ritual behavior there is an archaic and alchemic process occurring. It mixes and matches various types of behaviors to produce a superior, grand, or transformative experience. Ritual behavior is making connections. It has the ability to change the individual through the act of manipulations of energy, mood, and forces. Ritual thinking is very much a part of the process, and germane to alchemy. Thoughts and actions blend, combine, and collaborate. In this vein, thoughts and actions are energy generating, thereby leading to a possible mystical experience.

(Please note that this Chapter was taken from the book Myth, Ritual and Mysticism written by me, for Cognella Press)

# Shamanism

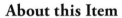

"Your mind is in every cell of your body."
Candace Pert, Neurobiologist

## About this Item

**Title**

There is no beginning and end in Barasana thought, no sense of a linear progression of time, destiny or fate

**Contributor Names**

Davis, Wade, photographer
Annenberg Foundation, funder/sponser

**Created / Published**

2009.

**Subject Headings**

- Barasana Indians–Spiritual life
- Amazon River
- Clothing & dress–2000-2010

- Religion–2000-2010
- Portraits–2000-2010

## Headings

Inkjet prints–2010-2020.
Photographic prints–Color–2010-2020.

## Genre

Inkjet prints–2010-2020
Photographic prints–Color–2010-2020

## Notes

- Title and notes from Annenberg Space for Photography exhibit spreadsheet.
- Theirs is a fractal world in which no event has a life of its own, and any number of ideas can coexist in parallel levels of perception and meaning. Every object must be understood at various levels of analysis. A rapid is an impediment to travel but also a house of the ancestors, with both a front and back door. A stool is not a symbol of a mountain; it is in every sense an actual mountain with the shaman sitting at the summit. A row of stools is the ancestral anaconda, and the patterns painted onto the wood of the stools depict both the journey of the ancestors and the striations that decorate the serpent's skin. A corona of oropendola feathers really is the sun, each yellow plume a ray.
- Copyright Wade Davis, 2009.
- Part of exhibit subdivision: Intro 1 and Ancient Wisdom.
- Use this credit line: From the no strangers exhibition 2012-2013, made possible by Wallis Annenberg and the Annenberg Space for Photography.
- Gift; Annenberg Foundation; 2020 (DLC/PP-2020:127-154).
- Exhibited: "no strangers: ancient wisdom in a modern world," at the Annenberg Space for Photography in Los Angeles, CA, November 17, 2012 - February 24, 2013; and at Kaneko, Omaha, Nebraska; and The Royal Botanic Garden, Edinburgh, Scotland.

**Medium**

1 photograph: color inkjet print mounted on foam core; sheet 100 x 69 cm

**Call Number/Physical Location**

LOT 15168, no. 77 (FM - MCD size) [P&P]

**Source Collection**

Annenberg Space for Photography Collection of Exhibition Prints, selected prints from the exhibition entitled no strangers

**Repository**

Library of Congress Prints and Photographs Division Washington, D.C. 20540 USA http://hdl.loc.gov/loc.pnp/pp.print

**Rights Advisory**

Publication may be restricted. For information see "Annenberg Space for Photography," https://www.loc.gov/rr/print/res/754_anne.html

Shamans are men and women who use alternate states of consciousness to assist them in healing and perceiving. Another name for a Shaman is a "Dreamer" and many are called in dreams; dreams can be an entry into this alternate dimension. Shamans have the ability to go into other worlds and bring back information. They are dreamers, prophets, and healers. These are extraordinary individuals who through dedication, faith, perseverance, and practice are able to tap into various metaphysical domains. Additionally, they use various purification methods to elevate and fortify their lives for service and power.

"The Shaman is the person, male or female, who in his or her late childhood or early youth has an overwhelming psychological experience that turns them totally inward. It's a kind of schizophrenic crack-up. The whole unconscious opens up, and the shaman falls into it. This shaman experience has been described many, many times. It occurs all the way from Siberia right through the Americas down to Tierra del Fuego." (Campbell, p. 107)

Shamanic practices are derivative of ancient and indigenous cultures, many of which are now extinct. Many have been preserved by their living relatives, anthropologists, and other researchers who through study, and observation, became convinced of the validity of their methodology.

Michael Harner, Malidoma Patrice Somé, and Carlos Castaneda are three such researchers. Michael Harner, the author of "The Way of the Shaman," highlights a number of central terms to the study of Shamanism. He begins his work by defining Ordinary States of Consciousness (OSC) as reality as it appears in a "normal" state and Shamanic States of Consciousness (SSC), which is extraordinary or non-ordinary reality. Shamans have the distinction to move from one state to another, at will. As researchers, students, and others, we must move beyond Ethnocentrism, which is an attempt to judge other cultures by one's own values and customs. Cognicentrism is a similar term, which is a belief that one's sense of reality is the only valid conclusion. Harner's first field work, as an anthropologist, took place in the Ecuadorian Andes in 1956 and 1957. From this research, he gains much of his knowledge of Shamanism from the Jivaro people. Later he studied the Conibo in the Peruvian Amazon. From these two cultures Harner acquired a body of his knowledge about shamanism. He cites his experience with a sacred drink made from ayahuasca, which caused a supernatural experience. He noted that there are other entrees into the SSC; it includes drumming (usually at rate of 205 to 220 beats per minute) using other instruments such as rattles, singing, and dancing.

In term of preferences, Shamans according to Harner, prefer to do their work in the dark, perhaps with a small fire. The quartz crystal is also used as a power agent and an energy conduit. Sometimes special herbs are prepared for the shamanic journey. Animals are viewed as guides and allies, and one is encouraged to find their power animal and nurture it.

Carlos Castaneda, an anthropologist from the United States, did his work in Mexico under the tutelage of Don Juan Matus who showed him the ways of his culture. Much of the Shamanic Practices of Matus involved the dreaming process. Another name for a Shaman is a Dreamer.

It is believed that many shamans are directed in their dreams as it relates to their shamanic work.

"I found out by means of my dreaming practices that a dreaming teacher must create a didactic synthesis in order to emphasize a given point. In essence, what Don Juan wanted with my first task was to exercise my dreaming attention by focusing it on the items of my dreams. To this effect he used as a spearhead the idea of being aware of falling asleep. His subterfuge was to say that the only way to be aware of falling asleep is to examine the elements of one's dream." (Castaneda, 1993, p. 35) Another aspect of Shamanism is energy work. Learning how to sense energy, deploy energy, and interact with it was also a major emphasis in Shamanic Practices.

Shamanism is not a religion, but a methodology to tap into the invisible realm. Some practice "sky gazing," which is a natural form of meditation. Some shamans participate in a vision quest, where they are separated from their group, and enter into an individual and solitary experience, usually for a three-day and -night period. During this time of seeking, listening, and contemplation, they obtain their mission and purpose.

"The vision quest is recognized as a practice for gaining spiritual guidance employed by early people living in the Central Plains of North America. Fasting, sun gazing, solitude, and other forms of physical deprivation were thought to grant the believer access to the spirit world. The guiding energy often came in form of an animal to serve the shaman as a connecting force—a link between the natural and the supernatural. Whereas among the people living in a verdant environment, it was the jungle spirits that capture a person and reward him or her with special powers. There were certain 'tests' that the person had to accomplish before being identified as a shaman regardless of the location and selection process. The tests might be physiological or psychological. They might result in a compromised physical condition or a state of mental disorder. Whether the maladies were the result of the selection process or the selection was the result of the spoiled mental and physical condition is unclear. Nonetheless, it was normal for the neophyte to experience a sense of rebirth or renewal whether physical or mental, and that encounter facilitated a spiritual linkage that was to be the basis for future shamanic practices." (Edson, 2009, p.45)

"The land is all-important, but the land is not uniform or generic. The land undulates and is specific. So the work that fashioned the land was particular, tailored, as is the character of the creative forces that a particular hill or valley reveals. The result is an endless map of spiritual opportunities." (Carmody & Carmody, p. 285)

"In the tropical forest of Brazil, among the Mehinaku, the most important belief is that many spirits shape the fortunes of the people. No beings are simply material; all are also spiritual, each carrying an insubstantial as well as a substantial form. Such insubstantial forms or spirits move like the wind, creak like the vines in a storm. These are the forces that visit the sick that the shamans see on their journeys that appear in every crack in ordinary material reality." "African indigenous religions often make an important place for the diviner, who ideally has access to the totality of knowledge. Using a scheme such as the 266 signs of creation. A diviner may sift a basket of 266 chits to determine what the future is likely to be or why a patient is suffering and ill." (Carmody & Carmody, p. 288)

"Dreams are important to most African Ethnic Groups, frequently because they bring the dreamer into contact with an ancestor who is functioning as a protector and source of counsel. Tribal kings wield sacred power, serving as links with the archetypal realms of the gods. The great gift of the African gods, and the great interest of African tribal religions overall is vitality, fertility, wellbeing, health, and strength to enjoy natural and human beauty and to resist illness, debility, and sadness," (Carmody & Carmody, p. 288)

According to Matus the energy body is the counterpart of the physical body; a ghostlike configuration made of pure energy, it can perform acts that are beyond that of the physical body, such as transporting oneself to the end of the universe. (Castaneda, p.31)

Malidoma Patrice Somé is a Shaman and the author of "Of Water and the Spirit" and "The Healing Wisdom of Africa: Finding Life Purpose through

Nature, Ritual and Community," in which he offers amazing insight into the Shamanic Practices on the Continent of Africa. He was born in a little village in West Africa named Dano, located in Burkina Faso, to a group of people called the Dagara.

"The Dagara people are well known throughout West Africa for beliefs and practices that outsiders find both fascinating and frightening. The Dagara connection with beings from the Spirit World has resulted in the accumulation of firsthand knowledge of subjects regarded in the West as paranormal, magical, or spiritual. Dagara 'science' in this sense is the investigation of the Spirit World more than the world of matter. What in the West might be regarded as fiction, among the Dagara is believed as fact, for we have seen it with our eyes, heard it with our ears, or felt it with our own hands." (Somé, 1998, p. 2)

(Please note that this Chapter was taken from the book Myth, Ritual and Mysticism written by me, for Cognella Press 2013)

# The Mystery Schools

## About this Item

**Title**

Former Broadway Trust Company, Broadway at Walnut St., Camden, 2003, The large classical building is now the St. James Apostolic Temple. It glows like a survivor from an ancient civilization

**Contributor Names**

Vergara, Camilo J., photographer

**Created / Published**

2003.

**Subject Headings**

- Banks–New Jersey–Camden–2000-2010
- Churches–New Jersey–Camden–2000-2010
- Recycled structures–New Jersey–Camden–2000-2010
- United States–New Jersey–Camden
- Storefront Churches

- Banks
- Time lapse
- Religion, Churches, church people, signs
- Time Lapse: Camden—NE corner of Broadway and Walnut St

## Headings

Photographs—2000-2010.

## Genre

Photographs—2000-2010

## Notes

- Title, date and keywords based on information provided by photographer.
- Forms part of the Vergara Photograph Collection (Library of Congress).

## Medium

1 photograph: color.

## Call Number/Physical Location

LC-DIG-vrg- 00274 (ONLINE) [P&P]

## Source Collection

Vergara, Camilo J. Vergara Photograph Collection.

## Repository

Library of Congress Prints and Photographs Division Washington, D.C. 20540 USA http://hdl.loc.gov/loc.pnp/pp.print

## Digital Id

vrg 00274 //hdl.loc.gov/loc.pnp/vrg.00274

## Library of Congress Control Number

2014648904

**Reproduction Number**

LC-DIG-vrg-00274 (digital file from original item)

**Rights Advisory**

Publication may be restricted. For information see: "Camilo Vergara...,"
https://www.loc.gov/rr/print/res/619_verg.html

## Mystery Schools

Mystery Schools were spiritual universities that taught their initiates how to tap into their higher selves and reflected on and pondered the mysteries of life and death. These universities sprang up around Egypt and Greece around the same time as the founder of Taoist Thought, Lao Tzu, was teaching Taoist Thought around China.

Mystery Schools revealed that through direct experience one could have access to higher knowledge and could experience a spiritual awakening. These sacred universities were a product of indigenous religious beliefs that had developed from primal shamanic roots, and from various ancient cultures from which they had regular contact. Incense of sandalwood was burned in the Greek temples. There were Buddhist monasteries in the city of Alexandria in Egypt, and a shrine in Athens to a Buddhist monk who set himself on fire in protest of the invasion of India by Alexander.

The word "personality" comes from the ancient term "persona," meaning a mask. Masks were used during ritual dramatic plays in the Mystery Schools. The secrets imparted to the initiates in these mystical rites was that the "personality" was no more than a mask, and behind this mask lay the soul, the "higher self," which the ancients called the "genius."

Mystery Schools were the birthplace of science and mathematics, rational philosophy, theater, the arts, and the Olympic Games. Mystery Schools were also the foundation of Western Civilization. Rites of the Mystery Schools were called initiations. These initiations included meditation, contemplation, confessions, purification baths, dramatic plays, festivals, and worship. The initiates dressed in white as a symbol of surrender and purification and they followed a vegetarian diet as well. The Initiations Rituals caused a shift in consciousness and awareness and was therefore a transformative process.

The body was honored as the temple of God and athletes were considered gods, as they could take their bodies to new heights, wherein they experienced an alternate state of consciousness. Mount Olympus was the site of many of their games and was considered the spiritual home of the gods. Mystical Yoga was also practiced. "Yoga" means "yoke" or "union" of body, mind, and spirit.

During their ritual plays, many would experience a catharsis, which means purification or transformation. Emotions were purged and these plays also were ways to encode their teachings into a story format. (Freke and Gandy)

(Please note that this Chapter was taken from the book Myth, Ritual and Mysticism written by me, for Cognella Press)

# Albert Einstein
## (1879-1955)

## About this Item

**Title**

Albert Einstein / Halsman, N.Y.

**Contributor Names**

Halsman, Philippe, photographer

**Created / Published**

[1947]

**Subject Headings**

- Einstein, Albert,–1879-1955

**Headings**

Photographic prints–1940-1950.
Portrait photographs–1940-1950.

## Notes

- Signed in white ink "Halsman, N.Y." lower right.
- Photographer's stamp "Photo by Halsman" on verso.
- Purchase; Rizzuto Fund; 1973; (DLC/PP-1973:313).

## Medium

1 photographic print ; 13 1/2 x 10 1/2 in., 34.2 x 26.6 cm.

## Call Number/Physical Location

PH - Halsman (P.), no. 3 (A size) [P&P]

## Repository

Library of Congress Prints and Photographs Division Washington, D.C. 20540 USA http://hdl.loc.gov/loc.pnp/pp.print

## Rights Advisory

Publication may be restricted. For information see "Philippe Halsman" https://www.loc.gov/rr/print/res/230_hal.html

Albert Einstein was a profound physicist and thinker, who struggled with the idea of what it meant to believe in God. He was the son of Jewish parents, who were born in Germany and for the most part considered themselves "entirely irreligious." They did not attend synagogue or adhere to the Jewish rituals. As a child Einstein did, however, have the opportunity to study the Talmud (a Jewish Holy book) and the Bible and was influenced by them, along with science, literature, and other ideologies. Einstein thought that the world was governed by laws and that was in and of itself awe-inspiring. Einstein's idea of God was one of harmony and beauty as it was expressed in the universe. He gave us the Theory of Relativity and upheld the Quantum Theory.

Quantum Theory holds that light and all forms of radiant energy were composed of discrete particles. There is a dual nature of light: it is both waves and particles. There is an inherent uncertainty at the sub-atomic level that observing a phenomenon played a role in determining its reality.

There is a probability and a chance factor in the way electrons behave. (Werner Heisenberg Bahr)

Einstein was looking for a deeper field theory or a unified or grand theory or theory of everything where he came to the conclusion, that all is energy! Einstein made mention of a phenomena he called "Spooky Particles" that are energy forms that appear not to respond to law, these particle appear to act on their own. Was he making room for the divine in this analysis?

He did suggest that there is more to the universe than law, as we understand it.

"At the beginning of modern physics stands the extraordinary intellectual feat of one man: Albert Einstein. In two articles both published in 1905, Einstein initiated two revolutionary trends of thought. One was his special theory of relativity, the other was a new way of looking at electromagnetic radiation which was to become characteristic of quantum theory, the theory of atomic phenomena, The complete quantum theory was worked out twenty years later by a whole team of physicists. Relativity theory, however, was constructed in its complete form by almost entirely by Einstein himself. Einstein's scientific papers stand at the beginning of the twentieth century as imposing intellectual monuments-the pyramids of modern civilization.

Einstein strongly believed in nature's inherent harmony and his deepest concern throughout his scientific life was to find a unified foundation of physics. He began to move towards this goal by constructing a common framework for electrodynamics and mechanics, the two separate theories of classical physics. This framework is known as the special theory of relativity. It unified and completed the structure of classical physics, but at the same time it involved drastic changes in the traditional concepts of space and time and undermined one of the foundations of the Newtonian world view.

According to relativity theory, space is not three-dimensional, and time is not a separate entity. Both are intimately connected and form a four-dimensional continuum, 'space-time'. In relativity theory, therefore, we can never talk about space without talking about time and vice versa. Furthermore, there is no universal flow of time as in the Newtonian model. Different observers will order events differently in time if they move with different velocities relative to the observed events. In such a case, two events which are seen as occurring simultaneously by one observer may occur in different temporal sequences for other observers. All measurements involving space and time thus lose their absolute significance. In relativity theory the Newtonian concept of an absolute space as the stage of physical phenomena is abandoned and so is the concept of an absolute time. Both space and time becomes merely elements of the language a particular observer uses for his description of the phenomena.

The concept of space and time are so basic for the description of natural phenomena that their modification entails a modification of the whole framework that we use to describe nature. The most important consequence of this modification is the realization that mass is nothing but a form of energy. Even an object has energy stored in its mass, and the relation between the two is given by the famous equation $E=mc^2$, c being the speed of light." PP62,32, Capra, Shambhala, The Tao of Physics

As I review the work of Einstein and attempt to put it in a perspective that is relative to my dream work, I have made the following observations. Dreams too have an energy field, what impresses me about dreams are the light and prisms of light expressed. Light is vivid, profound and awe inspiring. Motion and movement in my dreams, at times appear to defy gravity, space and time. The notion of mass is evasive and hard to quantify, but not solid, as in a non- dreaming state.

**Chapter taken from the Introduction to Myth, Ritual and Mysticism published by Cognella Press**

# Blocks to the Dreaming Process

**Self-Importance** -We take ourselves way too seriously, the ego can stand in the way of our development, as well as actualizing our potential.

**Self-Delusion** - Stay in touch with reality, especially as it relates to yourself.

**Anger- Anger and rage diminishes us at human being. Keep your peace.**

**Bigotry – Prejudging others and racism affects your Karma.**

**Greed** - Don't be greedy, take your share, and leave some for others. Greed is considered one of the seven deadly sins.

**Resentment – Don't be resentful or jealous. Remember, we will get our due, if we live according to principle and law.**
(Berg, Y. The Dreaming Book)

## Ways to Build your Capacity

> **Pray**
> **Read/Study**
> **Worship**
> **Doing good and helping others**
> **Exercise**
> **Detachment**
> **Humility**
> **Nature**

**Galatians 5:22...But the fruit of the spirit is...**
**Love**
**Peace**
**Longsuffering**
**Goodness**
**Faith**
**Meekness**
**Temperance...against such there is no law**

**(Berg, Y. The Dream Book)**

# About this Item

## Title

Sigmund Freud, 1856-1939

## Summary

Half-length, standing, facing slightly left; holding cigar.

## Created / Published

[no date recorded on caption card]

## Notes

- Photo by Williams & Meyer.
- This record contains unverified, old data from caption card.
- Forms part of: Sigmund Freud Collection (Library of Congress).
- Caption card tracings: Photog. I.; BI; Shelf.

## Medium

1 photographic print.

## Call Number/Physical Location

LOT 11831-A, no. 135 [item] [P&P]

## Repository

Library of Congress Prints and Photographs Division Washington, D.C. 20540 USA

## Digital Id

cph 3b20756 //hdl.loc.gov/loc.pnp/cph.3b20756

## Library of Congress Control Number

2003670023

## Reproduction Number

LC-USZ62-73426 (b&w film copy neg.)

## Rights Advisory

Publication may be restricted. For information see "," https://www.loc.gov/rr/print/res/118_freu.html

# Sigmund Freud

## Sigmund Freud (1856-1939)

Freud published the book **The Interpretation of Dreams in 1899.** By then he was in his mid-forties. Freud was also trained as a neurologist and had an interest in the causes of neurosis in the unconscious state of mind. Freud himself, went through self- analysis and was convinced that dreams play a great role in providing access to deep inner understanding. He believed that most dreams were repressed ideas or simply wish fulfillments. He felt that our deepest urges become more manageable through dreaming, as they serve as a key to the unconscious mind. (Fontana, 1991)

Dream analysis is one of a two layer approach (the other is called free-association) for uncovering unresolved psychological tension. This therapeutic approach is called psychoanalysis, of which Sigmund Freud is the father and foremost pioneer. Freud felt that dreams have two primary contents. One is called the Latent Content, which has coded symbolism and is what the unconscious reveals, and the second is called the Manifest Content, which is a clearer picture of what is going on and is a reelection of the conscious mind. His study and articulation in the area of dreams have been foundational and central to dream interpretation. In his view, the mind has three primary structures:

1. The ego or "I" which is self-conscious and self-aware. It controls the conscious mind.

    This part of the mind has a will and is relatively rational.

2. The Preconscious Mind is able to access facts, ideas, memories, and has motive.

3. The Preconscious Unconscious Mind stores repressed memories, unacknowledged wishes, conflicts, emotions, and urges. This is the part of mind that Freud calls the "Id" which is the instinctual and primitive state of mind.

Freud hypothesized that dreams are coded messages that reflect our expressed fears, impulses, desires, and our unconscious motives. Freud reasoned that through dream analysis these aspects of us can come to the surface so that they can be acknowledged and recognized and ultimately dealt with and resolved. (Hall, 1999)

## Sigmund Freud Offers the following assistance in dream work:

"Condensation is the superimposition of different elements on one another; hence, elements that are usually kept separate during waking thought may unite in a dream. Condensation results in over determination, i.e., each element may represent various dreams and thoughts of the latent content.

Displacement is the transposition of psychic intensity, affection, or significance from one element to another. As a result, an element that may seem to be of no immense importance in the dream may have the greatest significance in life and, conversely, significant elements in dreams may be of little importance.

Dramatization is the transformation of thoughts into situations and is, along with condensation according to Freud, the most important characteristic of dream work.

The symbolic function of dreams shows the no prosaic character of these mental processes and the non-logical quality of dreams. The dream is regressive with emphasis on the visual; logical connections are reduced to contiguity in space and time." (Kelly, 1991, p80)

Freud believed that every dream makes a demand on the Ego, either for satisfying an instinct, if it originated from the id, or for solving some conflict, removing a doubt, or making a decision. If the dream originates in the preconscious Ego, but the Ego is concerned with sleeping, it fulfills these demands with the "innocent fulfillment of a wish." This Freud calls the essential function of dream work. The dream, then is the guardian of sleep, while the needs of the Id and preconscious Ego are met through dream formations, sleep continues uninterrupted." (Kelly, 1991, p.81)

Significant to dream work is recalling, recording and participation. Having information of the elements and the processes involved in dreaming is also immensely helpful in dream proficiency, dream therapy, and its usefulness.

If we become lucid in a dream, we can intensify or deepen the message of the dream if we wish to, by consciously interacting with our dream imagery, asking the dream a question such as "What do you represent?," or "Do you have a message for me; or simply remaining present to the developing imagery and sensation." (Johnson, 2017, p.9)

# Carlos Castaneda

Noted anthropologist and mystic, Carlos Castaneda in his book "The Art of Dreaming provides deep insights into the dreaming process from a shamanistic perspective. A Shaman is a person who has the ability to go into other dimensions and bring back information. In his book, Castaneda tells of how he served as an apprentice with a Mexican Spiritualist named Don Juan Matus. Matus taught Castaneda about the role and nature of perception and how it works in shaping our world. Matus held that there is an unseen world around us of ancestors and spiritual forces that can be called upon through practice. He called people, who have the ability to interact with these force or energies, "Intermediaries."

Matus contended that our world, which we believe to be unique and absolute, is only one in a cluster of consecutive worlds, arranged like the layers of an onion. He asserted that even though we have been energetically conditioned to perceive solely our world, we still have the capability of entering into those other realms, which are as real, unique, absolute, and engulfing as our own world. (Castaneda 1993)

Having the energy to "seize them" and to make them accessible is the task at hand. Matus thought that this was possible through a process be called "energetic conditioning" He held that a practical way to achieve this conditioning is to put dreams to use and he offered a practical guide whereby this can be done. He felt that dreams are a "Gateway to infinity" and other domains of existence. He invited us to take this awesome ride, provided that we are ready and trained to do so.

For Matus, the most important aspect of dreaming is the experiences we encounter. This is not limited to just words, scenes and people but actual sensations and the awareness taken from the dream that that lives in our bodies and minds. Castaneda came to the conclusion, during his apprenticeship with Matus that "the human psyche is infinitely more complex than our mundane or academic reasoning had led us to believe." There are a myriad of energies that are unavailable to us due to our lack of belief, perception, and psychic energy. Additionally, one must be able to make the abstract concrete. This can be achieved through practice and fixation of the mind. We must have "freedom to perceive, without obsessions." (Castaneda p2)

According to Matus there are a number of actions you can take to build up your dream body:

1.  You must set up the dream. In setting up the dream you must stay with the themes of the dream and don't let it go. Focus on something specific. Concentration, integrity, seriousness and focus are required. In training and assisting in these areas Matus request, "In your dreams tonight you must look at your hand" In other words, you must pay close attention and looking at your hands tonight will requires your focused attention and energy, but don't worry, you have energy in reserve. During the dream process look around closely, take glances, listen attentively. This is exercising the dreaming attention

2.  The second step is centered on energy reemployment. Dreaming is an energy generating process. What is important during this stage is that we lose self-importance. We must humble ourselves and release the ego. Self-importance becomes a block and hindrance to the dreaming process. According to Matus, "most of our energy goes to uphold our importance. Don't get bogged down and don't fear. According to Matus, these guides will come to you and will teach and instruct you.

3.  "The third gate of dreaming is reached when you find yourself in a dream, staring at someone else that is asleep, and that someone else turns out to be you." (Castaneda, 1993.p.141) It is important

that you move around during this stage to keep the body fluid and in touch with itself. It is during this stage that the dreaming body begins to merge with the physical body. During this stage, you should be able to see and sense energy.

(Chapter taken from a book I wrote entitled A Dreamer's Joruney)

# Dreams as the Foundation of Religion

**About this Item**

**Title**

Guardian angel

**Created / Published**

Germany: [publisher not transcribed], 1914.

**Subject Headings**

- Angels
- Children playing
- Christianity
- Flowers

**Headings**

Prints.

**Genre**

Prints

**Notes**

- General information about the Popular and Applied Graphic Art print materials is available at https://hdl.loc.gov/loc.pnp/pp.pga
- Title information compiled by Junior Fellows, 2005-2017.
- Category designation on original folder: Religion - Misc.
- Title translated into German, French, Spanish, Italian and Turkish.

**Medium**

1 print: chromolithograph ; sheet 92 x 122 cm. or less.

**Call Number/Physical Location**

PAGA 7, no. 3828 (E size) [P&P]

**Source Collection**

Popular and applied graphic art print filing series (Library of Congress)

Dreams have played a vital role in the foundation of several of the major religions of the world:

# Christianity

In the life of Jesus, Matthew tells of Joseph who was engaged to Mary, was in a place of torment and distressed about her pregnancy which was unexpected. He was visited by an angel which told him the holy nature of the child's birth. In another dream following the birth of Jesus, an angel came again to Joseph, warning him that King Herod had plans to kill the child, and that he should take his family to Egypt to escape danger. When

Herod died, Joseph received another dream, that it was safe to take the mother and child back to Israel. (Innes, B.)

## Buddhism

In the case of Siddhartha Gautama, whose name was later change to Buddha, (which means the enlighten one.) His birth was also predestined in a dream. His mother Maya, related her dream:

"White as snow or silver, more brilliant than the moon or sun, the most beautiful elephant, with fine feet, strong and balanced, having six tusk hard and magnanimous has entered my womb." (Innes, B.)

## Islam

"Dreams have also played an important part in the development of Islam: the first part of the Koran was said to have been received from Allah by the prophet Mohammed in a dream, and the holy city Mecca was promised to the faithful in another. The Prophet paid close attention to dreams, and every morning he would discuss and interpret his own and those of his disciples. It was because of one of their dreams that the practice of the Muezzin, calling the faithful to prayer from the mosque was begun." (Innes, B. pp14, 15)

## Judaism

Ezekiel, according to scripture, had a shattering vision of God on a throne, which in effect left him unconscious. Jacob's experience with the angel, in which he proclaimed, "I will not turn you lose until you bless me." There are many accounts of the ancient Hebrews with angels, dreams, visions, and miraculous God interventions. Judaism is an extremely mystical religion where supernatural encounters were experienced on regular bases, which also forms and informs their myth stories, their rituals, their holidays, and daily lives. (Freke and Gandy)

There are 217 references made to dreams in the Jewish Talmud. Dreams were a foundational method of leading and directing prophets of old. One of the many accounts is of one of Joseph's dreams. "One day, Joseph told his brothers what he had dreamed. And they hated him; even more. Joseph said. Let me tell you about my dream. We were out in the field, tying up bundles of wheat. Suddenly my bundle stood up and your bundles gathered around and bowed down to it" Holy Bible Commemorative Partner's Edition Contemporary English Version, p44)

## Hinduism

"The earliest Hindu writing has little to say about dreams, but later religious text, known as the Upanishads, recognizes their importance:

"A man has two conditions: in this world and in the world beyond. But there is also a twilight juncture: the condition of sleep. In this twilight juncture one sees both other conditions, this world, and the other world. When someone falls asleep, he takes the stuff of the entire world, and he himself takes it apart, and he himself builds it up, and by his own bright light he dreams. There are no chariots there, no harnessing, no roads, but he emits chariots, harnessing the roads. There are no ponds, lotus pools and flowing streams, but he emits ponds, and flowing streams. For he is the Maker." (Innes, B.)

# Dreaming & Creativity

## About this Item

**Title**

"En aquella épocia había, pues, muy poca claridad ..." / Carlos Merida 1943.

**Other Title**

Estampas del Popol-vuh.

**Summary**

Print inspired by the ancient text Popol-Vuh, showing the evil Vukub-Cakix, and the two young gods Hunahpú and Xbalanqué who will bring him to justice, in the time of creation before light.

**Contributor Names**

Mérida, Carlos, 1891-1984, artist

**Created / Published**

1943.

**Subject Headings**

- Quiché Indians–Religion
- Quiché mythology
- Myths–1940-1950
- Creation–1940-1950

**Headings**

Lithographs–Color–1940-1950.

**Notes**

- In portfolio: Estampas del Popol-vuh / Carlos Mérida. Mexico: Graphic Art Publications, 1943.
- Print number 5 of ten prints, in portfolio No. 189 of 1000.
- Copyright by G.A.P., Mexico, 1943.
- Title from text quotation accompanying the print.
- Accompanying text in Spanish and English.
- Forms part of: Ben and Beatrice Goldstein Foundation Collection.
- Exhibited: World Treasures: Beginnings, Library of Congress, 2001-03.
- Accession number DLC/PP - 1998:153.1694d

**Medium**

1 print: lithograph, color ; 41 x 31 cm.

**Call Number/Physical Location**

NE2312.M47 A62 1943, no. 5 Case Y [P&P]

**Repository**

Library of Congress Prints and Photographs Division Washington, D.C. 20540 USA

## Digital Id

cph 3g11500 //hdl.loc.gov/loc.pnp/cph.3g11500

## Library of Congress Control Number

2003675378

## Reproduction Number

LC-USZC4-11500 (color film copy transparency)

## Rights Advisory

Rights status not evaluated. For general information see "Copyright and Other Restrictions..." (http://lcweb.loc.gov/rr/print/195_copr.html)

Robert Louis Stevenson was a Scottish Writer. He authored the book Treasure Island and indicated that most of his short stories came directly from Dreams. "Stevens describes how he came to complete one of his best-known stories, the Strange Case of Dr. Jekyll and Mr. Hyde: He recounts the following "For two days I went about racking my brains for a plot of any sort; and on the second night I dreamed the scene at the window; and a scene afterwards split in two in which Hyde; pursued for some crime; took the powder and underwent the change in the presence of his pursuers. All the rest was made awake, and consciously. (Innes, R. The Book of Dreams)

German chemist Friedrich Kekule had a creative vision. He was perplexed over the molecular structure of the compound benzene. "He knew it contained six atoms of carbon and six of hydrogen, but he could not work out how they were joined together. Then, as he later told a conference of fellow scientists: I turned the chair to the fireplace and sank into a half sleep. The atoms danced before my eyes...wriggling and turning like snakes. And what was that? One of the snakes seized its own tail, and the image whirled scornfully before my eyes. As though from a flash of lightening I awoke. I occupied the rest of the night working out the consequences of this hypothesis." (Innes, R. The Book of Dreams)

Musicians, also, have claimed to hear their compositions for the first time in their dreams, among them Mozart and Schumann. Richard Wagner said what he heard in his dream state became the leading motif of his immense operatic style the Ring of the Nibelung." Descartes dreamed that he found and read a dictionary and a volume of poetry…To Descartes, the dictionary represented science, and the poetry book represented philosophy. While in a dream state he believed he was visited by "the spirit of truth" and this spirit illuminated him. He concluded that his revelations were not the product of mind.

"Jasper Johns was supporting himself as a window dresser in New York City in the mid-1950s when he had a dream about painting an American flag. He acted upon his dream inspiration and that flag painting became part of a revolution in American art.

Salvador Dali's fascination with dreams was stimulated after reading Freud's Interpretation of Dreams, which he describes as one of the discoveries of his life. He attempted to preserve his dream Memory on Canvas and his remember for his work the Persistence of Memory.

William Blake's waking life and dreaming life were closely intermingled. How he valued his dreams is suggested by the titles of some of his work, such as Queen Katherine's Dreams and Oh, How I Dreamt of Things Impossible. His most specific acknowledgment of the inspiration he received from his dreams is found in a pencil portrait showing the facial detains of The Man Who Taught Blake Painting in His Dreams." (Van De Castle, p.11

The famous acrobat, Tito Gaona, stated in the April 8, 1974, issue of Sports Illustrated that "I sometimes dreamed my tricks at night and then tried to master them from the dream." P 15

"The Tsung Shu is an ancient Chinese almanac of life that has a nearly four thousand-year history. It contains a section on dreams called "Chou Kung's Book of Auspicious and Inauspicious Dreams" that dates back to 1020 BCE and was written by Chou Kung, a mathematician reputed to have assisted in the compilation of the I Ching.: (Innes, R. The Book of Dreams) P. 57

# The Sleeping Prophet

## Edgar Cayce
## (1877–1945)

Edgar Cayce (The Sleeping Prophet) lived in Virginia Beach, Virginia. He conducted a life of service that led him to being called the United States' most famous seer or mystic. He is one of the most documented intuitive who has ever lived.

While in a sleep-like state, he could see into the future, and into the present, and into the past. He had only an eighth-grade education, and by the world's standards, was a plain and simple man, but he had extraordinary abilities.

He was deeply religious and refused to use his talents for other than helpful and positive purposes.

Although the work of Cayce may be characterized in many different ways, perhaps the most important of those is his work in healing or health.

Cayce believed that sleep and dreaming were important to a person's spiritual, mental, and physical healing. In Cayce's readings he indicates that most of us need seven and a half to eight hours of sleep per night. We also need a certain amount of dreaming sleep. He felt that if we miss the last sixty minutes of sleep, we may very well be cutting down our dreaming by thirty percent. When we cut down on our sleep/dreams, we are cutting ourselves short of some of the mental, physical, and spiritual work that is vital to our overall well-being, because dreams are often a source of information, inspiration, guidance, creative insight, and spiritual experiences. The regular loss of dream time will contribute to the loss of some of these most valuable experiences. In addition to ensuring we get the proper amount of sleep, we also need to learn how to meditate.

Remember: "If we have trouble falling asleep or if we awaken during the night, we should remember the saying, "Why worry when you can pray?" (Cayce)

For Cayce, being healed or being made whole is a process of at-one-ment or becoming attuned, wherein the physical and mental are one with spirit. To be whole we must in accord with that for which we were created. We were designed to be in companionship and co-creator with the divine.

We must live dynamically and as a channel for the flow of spirit. Being whole is not a passive state, but rather an active and dynamic process. As physical, mental, and spiritual beings, we are endowed with many modes of functioning. We cannot think of ourselves as being whole unless we are actively manifesting these functions. Illness is being out of harmony and in violation of Spiritual Laws. Healing begins when our desires and choices move in harmony with the whole. Holistic healing results from balanced, integrated, and properly timed physical, mental, and spiritual applications.

A spiritual approach to healing acknowledges that God is the source of all healing and that all healing comes through the Spirit from within our own inner being. The term "spiritual" implies a constellation of considerations, including purpose, intent, desire, motivation, and ideals. According to Cayce there are two good reasons to be healed: A desire to change; and a desire to serve God and others.

Spiritual healing begins, for Cayce, when we reorient our desires, purpose, and ideals toward being one with and a channel for the flow of Spirit. The transformation occurs on the subatomic level, where the entering energy may bring the vibratory forces into the proper balance. There is within each of us a pattern, the law written through which we may enter into the very presence of the creative flow within ourselves. When this pattern is raised in one seeking to be a channel for the healing of others, it becomes like a magnet, which may raise the attunement of the one seeking healing. There must be an oneness of purpose. The recipient must be truly seeking a desire to be healed and to change. When one who seeks healing has set a spiritual ideal and requested help from others, the sensitive centers in the body becomes receptive and responsive to the help that may be received. This may come from a distance through prayer and meditation, or directly in the laying on of hands.

The laying on of hands was considered by Cayce as a powerful event. The laying on of hands is a type of energy work and a healing modality. Cayce thought that if the recipient has enough faith, there may be instant healing or it may be given over a period of days, weeks, or months. (Puryear, 1982)

Edgar Cayce (1877-1945) better known as the sleeping prophet was able to tap into the vast reservoir of knowledge known as the Akashic Record. This is a text is said to contain the very thoughts and actions of every human being that has ever lived.

"Edgar Cayce taught that dreams were the "safest way to enter this realm of unconsciousness. He even said that nothing occurs in our outer lives that was not already foreshadowed in our dreams." (Puryear, p.117) He referred to dreams as the gateway to heaven and the house of God. He emphasized that it was imperative to recall the dream to be able to truly benefit from the dream and he recommended the following to assist in dream recall.

1. Pre-sleep suggestion or auto suggesting to the conscious and subconscious mind to remember the dream.
2. Do not move the body upon awaking to remain in the dream state and position long enough to transfer the data.
3. Get the gist of the dream.
4. Use the essence of the dream in life.
5. Cayce hypothesized that human beings have a dual nature. It is important we allocate time each day to each area of our life, both natural and spiritual for balance and wholeness.

Cayce offers a number of recommendations for access into this realm of consciousness. Chanting or music raised the cosmic vibration level...

Breathing purifies, energizes and clarifies, allowing easier entry into the unconscious. Exercise and movement helps to open our chakras or energy centers located within the body. A straight spine is recommended for a better flow of energy throughout the human structure. Exercise is needed for strengthening the circulation and charging the electric energy in the body. Meditation and prayer are also recommended to open the portals to the divine or the cosmic realm. All parts of our being need some attention according to Cayce and none of us are totally balanced at all times.

**(Parts of this chapter is taken from a book I wrote, entitled A Dreamer's Journey)**

# Thoughts on Dreams

**"I want to know God's thoughts, the rest are details."**
**Albert Einstein**

*"In dreams we catch glimpses of a life larger than our own ...*
*thoughts are imparted to us far above our ordinary thinking."*
*Robert L. Van De Castle "Each of us has a dual life, both*
*sleeping and waking." Phyllis Baker "Life and Dreams are*
*leaves from the same book."*

*Philosopher Schopenhacier*

Question: Are dreams the results of our thoughts or are thoughts a result of our dreams?

The dream-self is an interaction of body and mind and spirit. Dreams can allow you to have a cognitive extravaganza. (Villoldo) There are no limitations to the inventiveness available to us when dreaming. Dreaming is the road into the infinity.

Stages of Dreams: What is REM? (Rapid Eye Movement)

Sleep is the gateway into our dream life. When the brain waves begin to drop to the alpha stage, one begins to benefit from the release of healing and reinvigorating hormones. Most experts believe that the theta stage is when most people dream. The delta stage is even a deeper level of relaxation. During this stage it is believed that one does not dream but the body is so still and relaxed it allows itself to be repaired and regenerated.

—Robert L. Van De Castle

During dreaming there is a suspension of time as we know it. This raises the question what is time? It is the eternal riddle. It possesses no solidity, so substance, no tangible properties. Dreams have given us a basis for believing that there is a nonmaterial component to our existence, as well as a continuity of existence that is not interrupted by physical death. Whether we realize it or not, we are dreaming our world into being. Dreaming is a way to make the best of our gifts and talents.

—Alberto Villoldo

According to Alberto Villoldo, our human mind experiences four states of consciousness: 1. Our ordinary waking one; 2. Dreaming; 3. Dreamless sleep; and 4. Lucidity when we are beginning to awake.

One way to enhance your dream life is to believe in beauty. GIVE UP UGLY STORES! Practicing beauty means recognizing what is pure and good in every situation.

For me dreams are metaphysical experiences, where sights, sounds, symbols and messages are communicated to the subconscious mind.

# Knowing

As we began to work with our dreams, a primary question that arises is "how do I know what is being revealed to me in my dreams is in some way true or significant?" The best way to know something is to experience the validity of your source and realize that we are multidimensional, multifaceted, and multi-intelligent beings. Research is now being done on emotional intelligence and I would like to add to this discourse another formulation of intelligence, and that is called intuitive intelligence. This realm of intelligence draws on the power of the subconscious mind, or your "G-d Center." The subconscious mind is that part of the mind that I believe is behind all that is conscious, all that is known, all that is manifested, what stands before and after, that which is visible and invisible.

The subconscious mind is activated by words, images, sounds, thoughts, and ideas. Faith, focus, and love all are seeds to help the subconscious have memory of itself. That is why creativity breeds more creativity, spiritual disciplines breed more spiritual power, and the process of thinking creates more and deeper and more profound ways of thinking.

Carl Jung thought that the way to selfhood is to overcome the fragmentation in our lives. We must pay attention to our attention, put the pieces together, begin to know ourselves in deeper and more meaningful ways. Jung also thought that the avenue to rescue ourselves and the self was to overcome the shadow, which is an archetype in Jung's Typology. The Shadow is the worst side of a person's nature. It contains egotism, narcissism, greed, evil remarks. Dream analysis can minimize fragmentation by confrontation and sublimation of the shadow, which can lead to the domain of growth and self-actualization. According to Jung, the ultimate goal for the individual is to reach for wholeness, balance, selfhood, and the cosmic level.

"Dreams act as a mirror to reflect our waking life."
"The unconscious moves in the direction of Individuation and Transcendence." Carl Jung

# What is Your Dream Goal?

A dream goal is to find your Internal Helper. Some ways to do so is to transform your messages or thoughts into pictures (auto-symbolic phenomenon); program your pre-sleep thoughts; and monitor your emotional states before going to bed and they can be transformed into visual symbols as well.

There is a variety of sensory stimulation that can affect your dream life. The following can assist in intensifying your dream life.

A. Music
B. Art
C. Poetry
D. Writing
E. Being in and surrounded by nature
F. Lectures, sermons and the spoken word
G. Reading
H. Movies
I. Gardening

It is vital to use also the power of imagination. Imagined satisfaction can have a powerful effect. By doing so, one can experience

A. Ecstasy
B. Intense sensual delights
C. Peak spiritual experiences

There is also a correlation between dreaming in color and creativity. The best candidates for dream therapy are those who have a spirit of adventure, a wish to explore the unknown, a rich curiosity about the range of human experiences; those who are self-aware and demonstrate emotional readiness and willingness.

Spontaneous healing is also associated with dreams. You may experience various encounters and guidance to changes in the diet or behavior. It is very important to pay attention to the instructions given.

Lucid dreams can be deployed to help you deal with troubling conflicts. Below are some recommendations to assist you in working with your lucid dreams:

    A.   Decide your response (more creative, more mature, more growth)
    B.   Enlist a dream figure to help you.
    C.   Build courage and self-confidence.
    D.   Do not commit "intrapsychic suicide"

Lucid Dreams are deeply cosmic. Our psychic growth can be recorded in the patterns of our past dreams. We must be careful not to trace old wounds. Sometimes some doors need to be closed! And we must learn how to overcome pain and hurdles. Turn your attention to the source of the dream who transcends body, mind, dreams, imagery, dreamless sleep, unconscious processes, and so on. Look for the light in your dreams, for light represents illumination.

Methodologies for Dream Interpretation

    A.   *Free Association (Freud) one must learn to build on words, themes, moods, and scenarios.*
    B.   *Dialogue (Gestalt) Begin to ask yourself or the dream characters questions: Who are you?*

    *Why are you here? Self-examination and awareness must be used.*

    C.   *Amplification (Jung) Introspection, expansion, and illumination.*

Phyllis Baker

*"If your dreams become too uncomfortable, you can always wake up." "Find your Dream print."*

*"There was always light shining in the darkness for those who dared to open their eyes at night."*

# Dream Assessment Questionnaire

1.  Approximately how many vivid dreams do you have each month?
2.  Have you ever had a dream that came true on some level? What happened?
3.  Have you ever had a recurring dream? What was it?
4.  Which people are consistently in your dreams? Why do you think so?
5.  Have you had a dream about or with a departed love one? Who was it and why do you think they came to you?
6.  Do you dream in color or only in black and white?
7.  What colors do you see the most in your dreams? Is this a favorite color and does it have meaning for you?
8.  Do you have artistic dreams? What are you doing artistically?
9.  Is there a sport that you are interested in or participate in during your dreams? What is it?
10. What language do you speak in your dreams?
11. Do you dream about a certain animal(s) on occasion? What animal?
12. Do you hear music or songs in your dreams? Do you recall any songs?
13. Do you have dreams of being out in nature? Any revelations?
14. Do you have dreams of being in a different place? City, state, nation, etc.
15. Do you ever have psychological or spiritual dreams? What revelations did you receive?
16. Are you a co/sleeper? (Do you sleep with someone)
17. Have you had a similar dream to that of a loved one?
18. Have you ever received a directive or instructions in a dream?
19. What are the general themes in your dreams?
20. Have you ever received a health-related dream? (Were solutions offered?)

21. Has your purpose/vocation been revealed in a dream?
22. What were the hobbies/passions you had as a child?
23. What do you find yourself doing the most in your dreams?
24. How do you reconcile your dreams? Do you take action?
25. Can you trigger/program or direct your dreams?

# Dreams, Visions, and Memories

## MY DREAMS, VISIONS, AND MEMORIES
## (In Poetics) by Phyllis Baker

Monday Night

She whispers in my inner ear and asks "Do you want to meet me"? My heart pounds in anticipation…I say yes, she directs me to go to the bathroom. When I return she is sitting on my bed in a yogi position, her countenance is bright, with a divine light over her head. She takes my hand and anoints me with power and love, and commands me to rest.

> (Song) Love lifted me; love lifted me, when
> nothing else could help, love lifted me.

Tuesday Night

I took a trip through what appeared to be a tunnel. I was moving faster than any plane, moving faster than the bullet train. I was sucked out of this dimension into the next…unrestricted by the laws of physics, not governed or hampered by time or space.

Wednesday Night

I hear the saints singing "take me to the water, take me to the water, take me to the water to be baptized"; as they move quickly through the woods toward a lake in North Florida, near Jacksonville. They are dressed in white, white sheets and towels cover their heads. The preacher man, with a towel around his waist, takes the lead of the song; before he baptizes the child, he sings "None but the righteous, none but the righteous, none but the righteous shall see God."… I linger behind the crowd, I am a child, and I strain to see and catch up. My mother yells, "Run, run, run!" I move up before the next baptism, and join the others in singing, "None but the righteous none but the righteous, shall see God."

### Thursday Night

I find myself in a church alone, but the preacher's voice is preaching through the walls, in his absence. I lie on the floor prostrate, in humble submission, I pray fill me lord, touch me lord, help me lord. Two questions are then posed to me:

1. Can you hear?
2. Can you hear music?
   (Song) "I heard the lord when the lord called me. When the lord called me when the lord called me."

### Friday Night

I am at a friends' house and we step out of the door into the back yard. The trees, flowers, even the dirt was alive. I say to myself, "they can speak, they can speak." … As they offer the secrets of their beauty, their essences, their healing power, I recognized that we are one and are helpers of each other.

*"Call on your Dream Allies to assist you in gaining access to explore the subconscious mind."*

Phyllis Baker

### Saturday Night

I see myself motionless and still with a white top and exercise pants. I called out to my physical body and say wake up, get up, wake up, get up, like Jesus calling for Lazarus … (Song) Rise shine give God the Glory… Rise shine give God the Glory.

### Sunday Night

I stepped in to Glory
"In my house there are many mansions" I experienced paradise…I saw indescribable beauty…fountains, gardens, colored lights, rocks, and

precious stones…The mansion was in dormitory style to accommodate many.

And the call came forth…teach, preach…teach, preach

And I said "Yes lord, yes lord from the bottom of my heart to the depths of my soul yes lord…completely yes, my soul says yes."

Dreams can be your spiritual media!

Dreams are your communication device with the divine!

Your dreams are your divine antenna!

Call forth your dreams,

Call forth your visions,

Call forth your Dream Allies!

Dreams are awesome! They have the remarkable capacity to take us through the wilderness of the unknown into the promise of the known. For too long many of us have fumbled through life in darkness in need of illumination, information, and clarity.

In a real sense the purpose of this book is to help us cross that bridge of isolation into the refuge of the solid ground of our thinking. Oftentimes we are in fact not on solid ground. We find ourselves sinking in doubt, confusion, uncertainty, worry, imbalance, sickness, and spiritual alienation. Your dreams can be your lifeline and guide back home. Your dreams are the bread crumbs the subconscious leaves behind, to guide you, and a way out of the limiting conditions into the oasis of light.

I believe that dreams have the ability (you have the ability) to connect to the subconscious mind (or divine mind) and therefore a linkage or bridge can be established to revelations. "Ask and it shall be given, seek and ye shall find, knock and the door will be open unto you." Dreams are your door to the information you need, the work that should be done, and possibly the key to your success.

In the dreaming and relaxation state, you are able to see, hear, move, react, and transform. In this realm there is unlimited access to knowledge and power. This information can provide insight into our lives that can lead to introspection, self-analysis, and wisdom. If we are successful in retrieving and interpreting the dream, transcendence is ours. There is information that we must carefully unravel. There are psychological dragons we must confront, there are flaws we must overcome, there are troubling thoughts we must put to rest. There is a past to be reconciled, there are people to forgive, and the first person on that list is you!

By paying close attention and understanding your dream process, access is available into a deeper realm of mind or consciousness, and therefore the unknown becomes known. The crooked places become straight, the intangible become tangible and therefore more manageable. At this point we must have the will, strength, and courage, the desire to prepare, to learn, to grow, to change, and to act. We all have room for improvement; we all can become better, healthier, and more engaged spiritual beings. This can be done by paying attention to and studying our dreams. Understanding our dreams also requires practice. This process should be practiced like a new instrument. Dreaming should be practiced like a sport you would like to master. This requires intentionality and consistency.

This book may be your breakthrough into the realm of the higher self— your best self, the master that lives in you!

# More of My Dreams and Revelations

**Title**

Our martyrs at heaven's gate

**Contributor Names**

W.J. Morgan & Co.

**Created / Published**

c1881 Dec. 8.

## Notes

- 15678 U.S. Copyright Office.
- This record contains unverified data from PGA shelflist card.
- Associated name on shelflist card: Morgan, W.J., & Co.

## Medium

1 print.

## Call Number/Physical Location

PGA - Morgan & Co. – Our martyrs... (D size) [P&P]

## Repository

Library of Congress Prints and Photographs Division Washington, D.C. 20540 USA

## Digital Id

pga 02234 //hdl.loc.gov/loc.pnp/pga.02234

## Library of Congress Control Number

2003672962

## Reproduction Number

LC-DIG-pga-02234 (digital file from original print)

## Rights Advisory

No known restrictions on publication.

# The Coronation A Visit to the Magical Kingdom

This was a dream/vision of extraordinary proportion. I witness the coronation of my aunt Gladys Sermons, a beloved, and saintly woman of God. My last aunt, a woman of excellent work, kindness, and hospitality. My aunt made her transition in 2021, and I was a witness of this phenomena. In this space, everything was bright and beautiful. My aunt looked so radiant, so spectacular in this domain. Dressed in white, to receive her crown, her reward, her welcome.

"Well done thy good and faithful servant, enter into the house of the lord."

In the dimension I was in, time does not exist as we know it, and as a matter of fact time seemed completely unnecessary. The laws of physics and gravity does not apply. Things were spinning, one moment something was here, then it moved, not a normal movement, but faster that the speed of light. It is said that light travel at 186,000 miles per second, things appeared to be moving faster than that, in this domain. The light stood out as something beyond any light we experience. In this space there is a divine glow, a radiance that is beyond compare. I do not know if this is the reception of everyone, but one thing I do know is that my aunt Gladys, was uncommon in how she lived and treated others. I do know that my Aunt Gladys love God and had an excellent spirit. Her ability and willingness to love may have had something to do with her reception in the kingdom.

# Dreams, Communion and Healing

I have never had a dream like this one! It was related to my Christian Experience and my Christian Tradition. On April 25, 2022, I was watching a Bishop from Los Angeles, CA give a sermon on the importance of the Holy Communion. The Communion Ritual is an important ritual in the Christian Church, but I never absorbed the full importance of it, as articulated by the Bishop/Prophet. The bishop indicated that he had a vision with Jesus and was informed that Christians don't really understand what his death, crucifixion, resurrection, and assentation, truly signified, and the many benefits we are entitled to as believers and followers. The bishop indicated that on the cross Jesus borne our illnesses, cured us of our diseases, and by his stripes we are healed. He went on to say that many sleep, (die) because the commandment or mandate is not honored.

I took what this Bishop said seriously, I follow him via television 3 or 4 times a week and for some reason I believe in him and trust his office as prophet. This Minister is from my Full Gospel Church Tradition, which believes in dreams and visions, holy visitations, the anointing.

(Intensified spiritual energy) and the like. After his Sermon, he called for a Global Communion, via television and I participated. I have had communion many times in my life, but this was different. Please be mindful that this program was tapped days earlier, during Holy Week, but its impact was the same.

I went to sleep that night, I had not been feeling well that past week, but I fell into a very deep sleep, and felt that I was being worked on and ministered to. When I awoke, the first thing I remember was the light show or light healing, with alternate colors of green and blues. In the book Aura-Soma: Healing Through Color, Plant, and Crystal Energy, indicated the following about green: "The spiritual meaning of green is Healing, Regeneration, Compassion. Love of the earth. The Emotional meaning is openness, calmness, freedom, generosity, and issues relating to the heart" Delichow, I. & Booth, M. (pp63, 64)

The authors went on to discuss blue: "The Spiritual Meaning: Blue is the color of the archangel Michael and of Krishna and Vishnu, two Hindu deities. They are described in the Bhagavad-Gita, one of the holy books in India, as living in blue bodies. This means that blue stands for Divinity, Water, (baptism, blessing, spiritual cleansing) (. P 65)

That morning I felt amazingly better, and over the course of three days, I had returned to my regular state of being, and above. This was the first time that I remember being healed in this way during the sleeping and dreaming process, and how so many things are important and significant. We miss out on so much, because we are not informed, don't believe and are not open to divine relations.

## Healing

Ancient peoples have discovered and utilized a number of healing methods, such as the use of herbs and other healing plants, spiritual readings, and other forms of spiritual healing, namely singing, dancing, music/sound making, and solitude are the ways in which the different healing modalities have proven beneficial and effective for unnumbered and untold generations and centuries. Healing is about directing and redirecting energy throughout the physical, psychological, and spiritual planes. Healing is about purifying and releasing negative and sometimes destructive elements that often keep us in turmoil. The ultimate goal of healing is to foster wholeness, with balance serving as the equilibrium that keeps and maintains the "whole person." The thing that is to be made clear is healing is based on faith and love. Therefore healing can be transforming.

Our bodies are energy systems of intelligence and vibrations. These cognitions and creative sources can be regulated, tapped into, and directed. They are also accessible for healing, for healing is a response to this magnificent energy exchange. The question then becomes, "What are the organizing principles for bringing healing into manifestation?" A principle is an overview of a plan or how something works. Below are some of the principles by which spiritual healing can transpire:

- **Anchoring**: Anchoring is making contact with infinite intelligence (God) the "Source," the "All." Ultimate reality is the unifying principle that guides all things. The anchoring process is connecting with this reality and remembering and believing we are a part of a spiritual universe and have input into the creative and healing process.
- **Visualization**: One must see through his or her mind's eye this power radiating through the entire being. It can be visualized as a powerful light, activity or movement, or an overwhelming excitement. For others it can be embraced as the "still voice" or the "Witness."
- **Shifting**: Shifting involves a change in consciousness where he or she identifies with the source, wholeness, power, strength, and is willing to take their rightful place in the spiritual universe of oneness, connectivity, and divinity.
- **Acceptance**: This is the stage where one receives his or her healing, by believing it is done, it is finished, and he or she is healed.

# The Laying on of Hands

The Laying on of Hands is a healing methodology that is known and used in many cultures and religious traditions around the world. It can be viewed as an example, or form of spiritual energy work, where energy is transferred from one person to another. In this type of healing, the healer covers the person seeking healing with his or her own healing or energy. In fact the healer heals him or herself and holds the "sick" person with his/her energy.

The laying on of hands is also a healing art discussed in the Bible and therefore also a Judeo-Christian tradition. As recorded in Matthew 8:3, "And Jesus put forth his hand and touched him saying. I will; be thou clean. And immediately his leprosy was cleansed." Pentecostal and "full gospel" (Fundamental Baptist, Church of God, Church of God in Christ, Spiritual Baptist, and Independent Baptist) churches use the power of the "Holy Ghost" as (an) "agency" by which they heal. On the other hand, in some of these churches, the minister places his or her hands on the heads of members as a way of healing through prayer after a segue from the "heat" of his/her sermon into their mode and means of healing. Here as with the other means, energy is crystallized in the hand and the hands are then conductors and transmitters of this abundant energy/soul outlet. In another instance, the laying on of hands is usually accompanied by a prayer, followed by hands laid on the forehead.

Under the Eastern practice of India, placing the hand or hands on or near the forehead is referred to as the "third eye." The third eye is believed to be one of the Seven Chakras or spiritual or energy centers within the body. Chakras are used in various traditions as points of healing within the body. Other cultures have different names for this methodology, such as "Touch Therapy," such as Reich, Massage, and Healing Hand. In some societies such as India and Japan, the body may not be touched; to encourage healing, the hands are merely placed close to various parts of the body.

Another chakra or point of contact for the laying on of hands is the heart chakra. This is considered the seat of the emotions. Many healers believe that emotional pain and distress can make the body sick; therefore, this center is generally included in a healing session involving the laying on of hands. On some occasions, the healer will use olive oil on the sick person. This is a part of the anointing process discussed in the Bible and other holy books. "Thou anointed my Head with oil, my cup runneth over." (23rd Psalm) Some groups put the three concepts of touch, prayer, and anointing with oil or holy water together in a healing session.

The Healer may speak in tongues during the healing session and the sick person may be asked to say or repeat something.

According to Christian teachings, the laying on of hands is first activated by faith in God. "Without faith one can do nothing" and a belief in the healer's ability to be used as a channel for healing. This ability is called a "gift." It is considered one of many available to children of faith or the body of believers. Others are the gift of teaching, prophecy, discernment, and music, to name just a few.

The healer generally began his/her sessions with a prayer of purification, thanksgiving, or a prayer of solicitation and invocation, where the spirit is invited to assist in the healing process. Sometimes the person desiring healing is giving a power object consisting of a piece of cloth or other objects that have been consecrated to wear for a certain period of time.

Touch therapy is now considered very therapeutic and useful in scientific and healing communities. The work in neonatal units in various hospitals throughout the United States is now embracing the use of touch with premature babies, and is discovering that human touch is life-enhancing.

Some have even described touch as being a "Human Requirement," necessary to sustain life and vitality.

On some occasions the healer will recommend additional remedies as well, such as a prescribed drink, of which water is the most common. The sick person may be asked to drink a number of glasses of water, or use garlic or the aloe plant to assist the healing and purification process.

As we recall the various healing arts, if one would like to use these methods, one must first heal their own negative conditioning regarding this methodology and beliefs about these sciences. We must be sure to record and remember these healing cures or these cures or methods will be lost. Healing is about relocating oneself with the larger scope of the cosmos and remembering who we are. We are spiritual beings living a physical life. All cultures have powerful resources that if explored may be utilized for health and well-being, for spirit is universal.

## Prayer

Prayer has the tremendous power to radiate energy in all directions. It sets in motion a series of events. It has been said that "you cannot think certain thoughts without evoking a certain response." Prayer, in indigenous cosmology, combines the power of faith, thoughts, words, and, very often, music. All of these are cosmic magnets and assist in bringing forth the invisible into physical manifestation. We live in an ocean of vibrating and electrically charged energy. (Blaze and Blaze)

Prayer activates the miraculous in our lives. Native peoples embrace nature-based religious systems. These ancestors intuitively understood the interconnectivity that unites all things. They were keen observers of the weather, the sky, and natural forces. They recognized these energy forces in animals, people, and the spirit world. It would be very easy for these animistic people to believe the idea of transferring one energy source to another. For many, life is a walking prayer. They hold the belief that sacredness can exist in many domains of existence. "Where attention goes, energy flows." Prayer is crystallized, concentrated thought. It is one's divinely focused and directed will. Prayer is a methodology that channels the flow of energy in a specific direction. Prayer is an act of faith, submission and love. Prayer is probably the most powerful and oldest of all spiritual disciplines. It is also the most misunderstood. Prayer transcends religion and culture, space and time. It belongs to all people and is at the heart of all spiritual ideologies and theologies. It binds people together as they seek to make contact with that "super-conscious force field that many refer to as God." (Blaze and Blaze)

Every word, thought, desire, sentiment, intention contains a quantum force field we call energy; every thought we have goes somewhere. A thought is not a non-entity, it moves; it has life, consciousness, and energy. We swim in a sea of energy like a fish swims in water. We do not and cannot exist without it. It is part and parcel of what and who we are. The more we understand this principle, the better prepared we are to embrace prayer and utilize its power in our daily lives.

When we pray, we activate electrical and vibrational force fields that encompass and envelop us. Prayer gives us access to infinite intelligence and strength. It is the "hook up" with divine mind. When we pray we ignite a series of events, and several laws and principles are activated on our behalf. (Blaze and Blaze)

A. The law of receptivity: "Give and it shall be given unto you." The desire and the act of prayer provide a channel whereby we receive. Giving of ourselves in prayer activates the law of receptivity. This is closely related to the law of cause and effect. When we give up our egos, give of our time, energy, and attention, we give of ourselves.

B. The law of desire: The law of desire propels and sets in place motivation. Motivation means to "move," to compel energy in a specific direction. Desire is that rush of power that intensifies and moves this energy. Energy cannot be stifled or stagnated when it's fueled with desire.

C. The Law of love: Love is a mighty power. Love is pure light. There is no force that can stand in the face of love, for love cannot be conquered. Love cannot be denied. Love purifies and cleans our intentions and as a result fortifies and propels us.

D.   The law of expectation: "And you will have whatever you say." Your intentions shape and cut into form and affect your thoughts and desires. Intentionality activates faith, and faith speeds up the process by cementing your intentions.

Many forms of indigenous spirituality are anchored and steeped in a profound mental science that was passed on from our ancient elders. The noticeable expressions of early spiritual traditions and their religious manifestations are largely physical, meaning that a great amount of movement, motion, and activity surround their expression. Let's not be confused that mental forces are not at work.

Indigenous religious systems are largely based in nature and the intelligence that resides in the natural forces of the earth and the solar systems. Astrology and astronomy tend to be at the heart of most religions. The wise men followed the "Star." The Islamic symbol is a crescent moon and star. The Star of David is the most powerful Jewish symbol. Isn't it interesting that many Christians worship on SUNDAY? We find astronomy throughout the religious diaspora.

Higher knowledge and wisdom is at the heart and soul of various global communities. Some scholars hold mental transmutation and alchemy as part and parcel of the ability to tap into and engage.

"The Source" or "Divine Energy." This is not child's play. This is the ability to integrate, assimilate, and demonstrate intelligence. Miracles, healing, psychic expressions, and the interaction with the spirit world are super-powerful phenomena. All is mind. All is intelligence.

(Please note that this Chapter was taken from the book Myth, Ritual and Mysticism written by me, for Cognella Press 2013)

# Meaning

## Viktor Frankel

The question of meaning is central to the study of Dreams. Society and humanity in general are built on meaning and how it is incorporated and assimilated. Meaning is the engine that makes the society run. Man's search for meaning is a central question, not only is sociology, but psychology, philosophy, and religion as well.

When we speak of meaning we speak of what gives your life significance, value, worth and purpose. Meaning can be viewed as even more important, that is meaning gives us a reason to exist, what helps keep us alive? I would like to raise a question? Is meaning generated, or produced, or is meaning revealed. Sociologists believe that meaning is constructed through interaction. The internationalist perspective or theory, is a primary theory of sociology. It holds that through interacting with others, meaning is learned, observed, and then modeled. This dance we engage in with others is developed and sustained in our relationships; thru face to face communication, by way of verbal language, body language, and through negotiating social contracts with one another.

Psychologists are interested also in human behavior, and personality. In the case of Carl Jung, the Swiss Psychologist, the father of the psychoanalytical theory, and the author of the book <u>Man and his Symbols</u>, suggests that meaning can be generated by religion, art, mythology, and cosmology. Carl Jung was also the architect of "The Collective Unconsciousness," which he perceived of and defined as <u>the library of the soul</u>, which is inclusive of our past, present, and future. This construct takes us to a deeper metaphysical stream of consciousness, that suggest that we can locate ourselves and meaning within our dreams, other subconscious, or preconscious channels. For some, this implies a cosmic realm of existence that is conscious and real, and in some cases verifiable.

For Jung, he thought that through self-exploration and connection to your higher self, or your real self, that meaning, purpose and direction can be achieved. The unconscious is revealed in this space of illumination, clarity, and meaning can be experienced and revealed. Meaning fuels our entire lives, it provides for us a life of stability, balance, passion, and purpose. Viktor E. Frankl was an influential psychiatrist from Europe, who authored the book **Man's Search for Meaning.** What makes his work so compelling is that he was a long-time prisoner in a concentration camp. In which he was stripped of everything. "His father, mother, brother, and his wife died in camps or were sent to gas ovens, except for his sister, his entire family perished in these camps. How could he ever continue; possessions lost, values destroyed, suffering from hunger, cold and brutality ;hourly expecting extermination, how could he find life worth preserving? A psychiatrist worth listening to. He, if anyone, should be able to view our human condition wisely and with compassion. Dr. Frankl's words have a profoundly honest ring, for they rest on experiences too deep for deception." (pp9, 10) "In the concentration camp every circumstance conspires to make the prisoner lose his hold. All the familiar goals in life are snatched away. What alone remains is "the last of human freedoms, the ability to "choose one's attitude in a given set of circumstances." This ultimate freedom, recognized by the ancient Stoics, as well as by modern existentialists, takes on vivid significance in Frankel's story"

(Gordon W. Allport, page 12, in the preface of Man's Search for Meaning)

It is so hard to fathom how one can find the psychological, or spiritual space, and will to survive, and still find meaning in life. Frankl writes," In spite of all the enforced physical and mental primitiveness of the life in a concentration camp, it was possible for spiritual life to deepen. Sensitive people who were used to a rich intellectual life may have suffered much pain (They were able to retreat from their terrible surroundings to a life of inner riches and spiritual freedom. Only in this way can one explain the apparent paradox that some prisoners of a less hardy make-up often survived camp life better than did those of a robust nature)" (p55, 56)

As it relates to the arts, Frankl discusses the role of art in one of his accounts. He recounts hearing someone playing the violin, and how he was able to take the music in and allowed it to provide a level of sublimation. He also states that "Humor is a weapon, for the flight of self-preservation" This opportunity for creativity and invention is the area of storytelling and humor was helpful in the self-preservation, thru entertainment. He mentions that this methodology assisted himself and another friend, by agreeing to draft an interesting story daily. "The attempt to develop a sense of humor, and to see things in a humorous light is a trick learned while mastering the art of living. Yet it is possible to practice the art of living even in a concentration camp, although suffering is omnipresent. To draw an analogy: a man's suffering is like the behavior of gas; If a certain quantity of gas is pumped into an empty chamber, it will fill the chamber completely and evenly, no matter how big the chamber. Thus, suffering is great or little. Therefore, the size of human suffering is relative." (p64)

Frankl holds that man search for meaning is the motivation in a person's life, the belief that rationalization is second. Meaning is individualistic and personal.

Dr. Frankel's theoretical approach for finding meaning is called: Logo therapy "According to Logo therapy, we can discover meaning in life in three diverse ways:

(1) By creating a work or doing a deed - Creating a work of art and doing a deed is inclusive of many things such as sewing, designing, poetry, authoring a book, painting, dancing, gardening, starting a study group, organizing an event for children, coaching a little league group, cutting the grass of a senior, or incapacitated person. In this vein, there are a multitude of opportunities to accomplish this method, to acquire meaning.

(2) By experiencing something or encountering someone- Frankel, thought that love is the greatest power on earth. He thought that

love was so powerful, that even though his wife was separated from him during the holocaust, his love for her sustained him, even though he found out later that she was deceased. This even pointed to the fact that love can survive death. By encountering someone, it is possible that this meeting or encounter will change the trajectory of your life, and of course, give your life meaning. There is something immensely powerful about experiences. There are some experiences that can profoundly impact your life. One can experience the birth of a child, experiencing your parents, family members and friends. Additionally, on a lesser level a hobby, a concert, a performance, a tour of a garden. Think also of travel. International Travel has had a profound impact on me, my world view, and my appreciation for all of humanity.

(3) By the attitude we take toward unavoidable suffering- The true measure of a man is how he or she manages demanding situations. For Frankel, in these moments, or seasons of suffering, a person truly defines themselves as who they really are, what they truly believe, their perseverance, and their ultimate hope. From the vantage point of suffering, the soul gains strength, grace, and meaning.

The two psychologists mentioned, provide examples of how meaning can be achieved. I would like to provide an additional strategy of finding meaning. I believe that meaning can be found in self-exploration, by exploring, testing, experimenting with ideas, methods, arts, potential hobbies, skills, diverse people. Something will speak to you. Paths will be illuminated, passions will be explored. To be a master of self requires diligence, focus, concentration, and knowing yourself, or having some knowledge of yourself, and your presence.

# Carl Jung

## About this Item

### Title

[Carl Gustav Jung, full-length portrait, standing in front of building in Burghölzi, Zurich]

### Created / Published

[ca. 1909]

### Subject Headings

- Jung, C. G. – (Carl Gustav), – 1875-1961

### Headings

Photographic prints–Hand-colored–1900-1920.
Portrait photographs–1900-1920.

### Genre

Portrait photographs–1900-1920
Photographic prints–Hand-colored–1900-1920

### Notes

- Exhibit loan 4058-L.
- Unprocessed in PR 13 CN 1976:115.3

**Medium**

1 photographic print: hand-colored.

**Call Number/Physical Location**

Unprocessed in PR 13 CN 1976:115, no. 3 [P&P]

**Repository**

Library of Congress Prints and Photographs Division Washington, D.C. 20540 USA

**Digital Id**

ppmsca 07205 //hdl.loc.gov/loc.pnp/ppmsca.07205

**Library of Congress Control Number**

98514811

**Reproduction Number**

LC-DIG-ppmsca-07205 (digital file from original)

**Rights Advisory**

Rights status not evaluated. For general information see: "Copyright and Other Restrictions ...," https://www.loc.gov/rr/print/195_copr.html

# Carl Jung

Jung gave us the term "Individuation" and defined it "as the conscious coming to terms with one's inner center," he called it the psychic nucleus. For Jung, individualization is possible when the self is discovered. The self, for Jung is the inner guiding factor. This is different from the conscious personality and can only be grasped through the investigation of one's own dreams and the discovery of information that exists in the unconscious reality.

Dreams can contain valuable information that can assist in reaching inner growth, integration, and fulfilling ones destiny. This is the greatest human achievements. Exploring the unconscious through dreams can provide a bridge or link between the conscious and unconscious states of mind. It is recommended that one must become bilingual with dream language and study it as though studying a foreign language...consistently, diligently, and practically. It is imperative that we practice our dream language.

The purpose of paying attention to one's dreams is to restore psychological balance. Jung felt that not only must fragmentation (our broken parts) be overcome, but also the shadow. The shadow is described as the worse side of human nature. The shadow is the dark side of a person's psyche it contains egoism, mental laziness, plots, schemes, carelessness, love of money, and possessions, evil remarks, fear, and cowardliness. Some people feel compelled to live out their worse side, and ultimately it will cause themselves, and others pain.

Dream analysis can minimize fragmentation by confrontation and a process called sublimation of the shadow which can lead to the domain of individuation and self-actualization... Dreams can move one to the light, for the ego needs clarity, strength, and honest self-examination.

Reorganization is a path to the cosmic human being...the best in each of us.

The ultimate goal for the individual is to reach for self-realization, integration, selfhood, and individualization and wholeness (Jung, 1964)

Jung is also remember for offering the **Seven Major Archetypes** as aspects of ourselves that appear in our dreams. They are as follows:

**The Wise Old Man-** This archetype can also be presented as a woman and was called the "mana personality". It is a primal source of vitality and growth that can heal but also damage. The wise old man may appear as a professor, priest, and sometimes a teacher. It is quasi-divine and can be used to lead one towards or away from the higher level of development.

**The Trickster-** The Trickster is full of tricks, jokes, and pranks and may appear in dreams as a clown or sinister figure. The trickster is over playful to the point that he or she can interrupt and spoil pleasure in a dream.

**The Persona –** The Persona is the mask that we have reconciled ourselves to, and can be very dangerous if identified with too much. This is the self that we present to the outside world.

**The Shadow-** The Shadow represents the dark side of human nature, and Jung gave Freud credit for introducing what is referred to as the "abyss of human nature." The shadow is selfish, brutal, and uncivilized. This part of the personality cannot be fully disguised and must be tamed, integrated and harmonized into the personality.

**The Divine Child-** represents the true self and includes innocence and vulnerability. It generally appears as a baby or infant and can put the ego back in place because the child humbles the self, and helps to negate arrogance and narcissism from the personality.

**The Anima and Animus**-The Animus represents the masculine aspects and qualities of being and the Animas represents the feminine qualities. Jung asserted that both aspects are within, and lead to fully exploring what is generally unexplored. If not recognized, it can lead to a stymied human potential, or to over-emotionalism, or ruthlessness and destruction.

**The Great Mother**-The Great Mother plays a pivotal role in spiritual development. She is earthy, yet divine, and embodies feminine mystery and power. She is fierce and nurturing, gentle, yet strong. She serves to assist in psychological integration and development. The Great Mother is also a protector, for she watches over and cares for the child.

Dreaming can help one to regain composure, and to rejoin the self. Jung reminds the dreamer to be "prepared for confrontation." We must also remember that the healing process comes out of the individual; no one can impose growth upon another. That person must agree to be engaged. Keep in mind that introspection, and self-knowledge is the goal. (Jung, 1964)

## The Collective Unconscious

For Carl Jung, the Collective Unconscious goes beyond the Personal Unconscious (which are those aspects from the personal psyche). It is based on firsthand experiences that have now become unconscious because they have been forgotten, not intense enough to be remembered, or have lost their importance) (Kelly)

"As Jung observes, the collective unconscious seems to consist of primordial motives or images of the kind found in myths. This Jung, could infer, following his exhaustive study of mythological tales. The universality of these myths indicated that the collective unconscious transcends individual experience. (Kelly, 1991, p.115)

Jung felt that this library of the soul, this inherited cosmic space is available, and is an avenue that can be experienced in your dreams.

## Symbols

Symbols stand for something more than what it appears. It is more meaningful than a sign, because signs represent the full value, or the meaning is less significant to the psyche." Symbols, moreover, are natural, and spontaneous products. No genius has ever sat down with a pen or a brush in his hand and said, "Now I am going to invent a symbol." In dreams, symbols occur spontaneously, for dreams happen and are not invented; they are, therefore, the main source of all our knowledge about symbolism.

Symbols, I must point out, do not occur solely in dreams. They appear in all kinds of psychic manifestations. There are symbolic thoughts and feelings, symbolic acts, and situations. It often seems that even inanimate objects cooperate with the unconscious in the arrangement of symbolic patterns." (Jung, 1964, p.4)

"There are many symbols, however (among them the most important), are not individual, but collective in their nature and origin. These are chiefly religious images. The believer assumes that they are of divine origin, that they have been revealed to man." (Jung, 1964, p.41)

## Synchronicity

Synchronicity, as defined by Carl Jung as divine coincidences. According to his view of synchronicity, there are things that don't just happen, they are preordained, predestine, or meant to be. There is a larger, and greater plan or planner at work.

When I was a child, it seemed to me I could make magic, by using the law of belief (Faith) and the law of desire. Things, money, and opportunities just seemed to come my way. Not only as a child, but also as an adult. I remember vividly at the age of about seven or eight, my mother lost the diamond in her wedding ring. My mother was very sad about this, it was obvious to me that she was sad and disappointed. I remember being in the kitchen and I said to myself, I am going to find that diamond. It was a tiny diamond, and the ideas of her finding it again, seemed almost impossible. During the week of the missing diamond. I found the diamond attached to my pajamas. I could have dismissed the connection of the tiny diamond I was a young child, but something told me that this was the diamond my mother lost. She lost it in the wash, it could have stayed in the washer, and washed away in the rinse, but it didn't, I have four siblings, the little diamond could have been attached to one of their clothing, but this find was for me; because I wanted to be the one to find it, and I believed that I could.

# Other Great Minds

I have included in this section lesser known individuals, that have made an impact on the world, and within their sphere of contact. These individuals have not necessarily written or spoken extensively on dreams, but were dreamers, and had very deep insight, revelations and manifestations. Those included were great spiritual and intellectual beings. In this part of the book, I pay homage and respect to these individuals who have left their mark on many, and their ideas, and inspiration should not be forgotten.

Included in this section is the late Charles Fillmore, teacher, minster, and healer. Emile Cady, metaphysician, minister, teacher and healing. The Reverent Mary Tumpkins, minister and teacher of the Universal Truth Center, and my own mother, Zenovious Stripling, Evangelist and teacher in the Church of God in Christ.

## Charles Fillmore

Charles Fillmore (1854–1948) was a foremost scholar, theologian, and spiritual practitioner. He, with his wife, and collaborator Myrtle, co-founded the largest New Thought Organization in the country: The Unity School of Christianity whose major headquarters is located at Unity Village, in Kansas City, Missouri. Fillmore was central in articulating and formulating the New Thought message, which at its heart promotes a practical form of Christianity. "These teachings focused on spiritual truths, the nature of God, the laws of man's being, manifesting the Divine within, and the spiritual practices that facilitated it. These practices included the use of intuition, strong faith, powerful ideas, thoughts and words of affirmations and denials, going into the silence and prayer. The Basic Unity Teaching also contained doctrinal statements on bodily regeneration, human perfectibility, the afterlife, reincarnation, and the practice of metaphysical healing." (Vahle, 2008; p. 9)

## The Nature of God

"Charles's views on the nature of God formed the basis upon which his doctrine was developed. He acknowledges that God was 'Omnipotent, Omniscient, and Omnipresent.' Nevertheless, he did not see God as many traditional Christians viewed God—as a mighty king, decreeing the destiny of man with an iron hand, from which anger is dispensed more freely than love." (Vahle, p. 11)

Charles Fillmore took the view that God is again omnipotent, meaning that God is all powerful. This power is made manifest through Spirit, and Fillmore defines God as spirit, as man is spirit, and in this vein we share a divine relationship, in which communion and fellowship with God is natural and accessible. Fillmore departed from Traditional Christianity in terms of how the power of God is distributed, in that man, through his spiritual birthright, is powerful as well. This invisible spirit and power is not separate from us but is in and all around us. Fillmore's view of man empowers him and encourages him to own his own power, and along with that power is the responsibility to be all we are meant to be as sons (children) of God. Along these lines, God is omniscient, meaning that God is all-knowing; by acknowledging, tapping into and owning, this truth, we are heir to the knowledge and the intelligence of the Father (God); Divine Ideas and information are ours as well and are manifested and demonstrated in our world, life, and affairs. The third of the trilogy is omnipresence, meaning that God is equally present. It also holds that we don't have to wait for God to come, for God is with us always, right here, and right now.

Fillmore believed that God is an invisible spirit that is all-loving, all-powerful, equally present, all-knowing, and we as God's children are commissioned and empowered. In this view, we should no longer see ourselves as helpless victims, but as a part of the Godhead; and as such, we are strong, intelligent, and powerful. Additionally, the ideas of a punishing God who is ready to throw us in hell is wiped away and replaced with a God of love.

## Manifesting the Divine Within

"Charles recognized that, while the power of the divine lies within humankind, most men and women had not manifested that power. The 'Indwelling Presence' was latent within them, existing in potential only. Men and women could manifest the Inner Divinity or Christ within by (1) understanding spiritual truth, (2) living in accordance with the laws of man's being, and (3) understanding the spiritual practices contained in the Basic Unity Teaching." (Vahle, p. 14)

Fillmore viewed Jesus as a highly developed spiritual being, who was able to manifest the perfect ideal of manifesting the divine within. He thought that Jesus was fully human; therefore providing for us a great example of what was possible for us.

## Regarding the Teachings of Jesus

Jesus taught a message that was vibrant, full of life, love, and the power of God. Fillmore founded that most in the traditional churches were not true followers of Jesus the Christ. Many were Christians in name only but lack the fervor and zeal of Jesus. Many had become dry and lifeless individuals.

"As men and women manifested the Christ within, they demonstrated spiritual truth. These demonstrations included physical and psychological health, prosperity, and success in work and relationships. Those who fully manifested the Indwelling Presences regenerated their bodies. Charles considered these demonstrations of spiritual truth as living proof of the correctness of the Basic Unity Teachings. Charles called this teaching 'The Truth' because of his convictions that the truth had been discovered about

95

how men and women could manifest the divine potential that was inherent in their nature." (Vahle, p. 15)

## Regarding Metaphysical Healing

Fillmore felt that the church of today has lost much of its power. In Biblical times, the priests, spiritual leaders, and people of the early church practiced the laying on of hands, had visions and revelations, raised the dead, and were indeed workers of miracles. In truth, many of the churches of today have come up short in the spiritual practices that made this religion powerful and rich in spiritual traditions that edified the body of God, and provided relief for many of the ills that plagued the people. Fillmore was concerned that the church people had not used their God-given potential, and was lacking in terms of reaching the mark set and established by Jesus.

## Bodily Regeneration

"Charles believed that, if men and women fully manifested the Christ within, they could regenerate the cells of their bodies, live far beyond the normal life span, and overcome physical death. In April 1889, in the inaugural issue of Modern Thought magazine, he expressed confidence in the ability of humans to regenerate their bodies." (Vahle, p. 24) "He came down with them and stood on a level place, with a great multitude of people from all Judea, Jerusalem, the coast of Tyre, and Sidon. They had come to hear him and to be healed of their diseases; and those who were troubled with unclean spirits were cured. And all in the crowd were trying to touch him, for power came out from him and healed all of them." (Luke 6:17-19)

Fillmore thought that healing can be accomplished through soul concentration, awakening the power within, and following Jesus by raising our spiritual consciousness through prayer; to such a level we make contact by meditation, affirmations, denials, and conserving sexual energy. (Vahle, pp. 26, 27)

## Regarding Church Organization

Fillmore felt that the traditional church with its dogmas and creeds is not the church that Jesus left behind. Fillmore held that Jesus did not impose the doctrines, creeds and practices that are commonplace in today's churches. Jesus was known as a law breaker, which implies that many of the laws of the clergy weren't all that important to Jesus.

"On another Sabbath he entered the synagogue and taught, and there was a man there whose right hand was withered. The Scribes and the Pharisees watched him to see whether he would cure on the Sabbath, so that they might find an accusation against him. Even though he knew what they were thinking, he said to the man who had the withered hand, 'come and stand here.' He got up and stood there. Then Jesus said to them, 'I ask you, is it lawful to do well or to do harm on the Sabbath, to save life or to destroy it?'"(Luke 6:6-9)

Jesus' agenda was to do good work, and to honor God. Fillmore thought that this should be the agenda of the church as well.

The church we see today is, in the analysis of Charles Fillmore, largely a business or an industry whose primary function is to maintain a profit, a power base, and status in the community.

What would Jesus do or think about the churches of today? Have they been compromised, diluted, or lost the original intent or function? Fillmore must have found these issues troubling. He attempted to point us back to the original intent of the church as a true place of learning, worship, and fellowship.

## Regarding the Afterlife

Charles Fillmore's view of the afterlife is different from many of those in traditional Christianity. He did not believe in a Heaven in the sky that people go to when they make their transition, therefore the traditional Heaven and Hell framework was not a part of Fillmore's belief system.

Traditional Christians believe that if you are a good person, and accept Jesus as your Lord and Savior, you will spend eternal life in heaven, and most are taught that heaven is a place in the sky. Adversely, if you were a bad person and did not accept the Lord Jesus as your personal savior, you will spend eternity in Hell, where you will be consumed by eternal fire and damnation.

Charles felt that death was not real, but or an illusion; he believed in a higher order of life that has no bounds.

# Reverent Mary Tumpkins and The New Thought Movement

There are a growing number of African Americans who are attracted to the Christian New Thought Movement. This chapter explores and summarizes some of its concepts and beliefs.

For each of the world's major religions, there is a corresponding mystical tradition. The New Thought Movement is the mystical arm of Christianity. According to Charles Fillmore, founder of the Unity School of Christianity, New Thought is "A mental system that holds man as being one with God (good) through the power of constructive thinking" (*The Revealing Word*, 140).

Always inspired by her messages, I conducted an interview with Dr. Mary Tumpkin, a leader in the Christian New Thought Movement and gained tremendous insights from her.

The New Thought Movement offers an alternative to fundamental Christianity. It is the reinterpretation of Christian concepts, themes, ideas, and scriptures from a historical, practical, and personal perspective. New Thought Christians, like all mystics, seek individual communion with God. The Bible is studied allegorically as the universal story of humankind. This is a liberating theology that strives to understand an ultimate reality (GOD) that is good, omniscient, omnipresent, and omnipotent. New Thought shuns religious dogma in favor of principles for empowered living.

The New Thought Movement follows the teachings of Jesus, who is recognized as a "Way Shower" or model rather than as the Savior of traditional Christianity. According to New Thought, Jesus' message was one of peace and love, and it promoted the development of a personal relationship with God. Jesus taught that people had the power to tap into God for themselves, and during his life he demonstrated how this could be done. The New Thought Movement teaches that God is neither a person, place nor thing, but invisible energy which permeates all that is. The best possible description of God for the New Thought Christian is the "Absolute." Possible alternative words for God are Divine Mind, Being, Creator, Source, and Spirit.

Although the New Thought Movement began less than one hundred years ago in the United States, its true origin dates as far back as the Mystery Schools of Ancient Egypt and Ancient Greece. In fact, it embraces much of the scholarship, philosophical thought, and foundational ideas of various Eastern religions. Some early New Thought pioneers include: Phineas Parkhurst Quimby, who is generally credited as the father of New Thought. Quimby was born in New Hampshire and is remembered for his work in mental healing and his technique of hypnotism; Mary Baker Eddy, the founder of Christian Science, was a noted writer, thinker, and healer; Emma Curtis Hopkins was another contributor, and she was the founder of the Christian Science Theological Seminary in 1887; Charles and Myrtle Fillmore were the founders of the Unity School Of Practical Christianity; Ernest Holmes and his brother Fenwick started the Metaphysical Institute in 1917, and in 1926 Ernest published the book *Science of Mind*; Dr.H. Emile Cady was one of the first prominent writers of the Unity Movement, and she wrote clear lessons of healing.

The New Thought Movement draws from many roots, including Gnosticism (Christian Mysticism). Gnosis means "knowledge," and the Gnostics believed they were the bearers of the secret teachings of Jesus. The Gnostic Gospels are gaining visibility in contemporary society, especially since the discovery of the Gospel of Thomas in a cave in Nag Hammadi, Egypt in 1945. Among the Gnostics, women were just as important as men, and many women were profound teachers, priests, and healers. Many of the leaders of the contemporary New Thought Movement are, in fact, women.

Ancient Judaism, the mother religion of Christianity, is another strong root of New Thought. Judaism allows for the allegorical interpretation of the scriptures. The Jewish Mystical Tradition is called "Kabala," which means "tradition." Its ultimate goals are to get closer and closer to the one great essence and to understand that duality of knower and known does not exist—there is no separation at all. Kabalists practice yoga, utilize methods of breathing and concentration, and repeat mantras as methods of reaching spiritual revelation

The Buddhist tradition has made its mark on New Thought as well: the New Thought Movement embodies the "Eight Fold Path" that comes out of the Four Noble Truths of Buddhism. Although Buddhism began in India, it is rare there today. It has since moved east to Japan, China, Tibet, and other places within and around the Asian Diaspora.

Perhaps the oldest, most far-reaching roots of New Thought Christianity can be traced to the ancient Mystery Schools or Spiritual Universities of Alexandria, Egypt and Greece. The Mystery Schools arose from ancient Shamanic practices and involved the study of rational philosophy, music, and art. They were also the birthplace of science and mathematics. Pythagoras, the Father of Mathematics, was initiated into and studied in the Mystery Schools for twenty years. The famous saying "Know Thyself" was inscribed over the portals of the temples.

The Mystery Schools taught that life is a process of awakening. Masters stressed the importance of finding one's higher nature and the underlying oneness with God. In laymen's terms, they were interested in the development of the whole person. These schools accepted a personal and spiritual understanding of life that promoted integration, self-realization, and self-actualization. Initiations stressed focus, concentration, study, readiness skills, and mastery, which were believed to be the keys to spiritual power and mind control. The masters understood the danger of mixing higher knowledge with unready minds and consciousnesses. Many of the same concepts can be found in the New Thought Movement today.

According to the Reverend Dr. Mary A. Tumpkin, President of the Universal Foundation for Better Living (an international association of New Thought Christian churches and study groups founded by the Reverend Dr. Johnnie Coleman in 1974), and Senior Minister of the Universal Truth Center in Miami Gardens, Florida, one of the missions of the New Thought Movement is to bring the female back to the Christian dialogue. Says Tumpkin, "New Thought is feminism in action." Another of the Movement's missions is to offer "a counter discourse to mainstream Christianity and a larger look at the Christian religion, other world religions, and spirituality in general. It does so by drawing of a divergent set of ideas and theoretical perspectives." Tumpkin encourages individuals to find their own unique truths as they search out God's plan for their lives.

"Ultimately, the New Thought Movement must work to build and establish a community of faith that upholds spiritual unfoldment, personal growth, equality, scholarship, and goodness," she says.

Dr. Tumpkin sees the New Thought Church as a response to the victimized and suffering church. "It offers itself as new model: an empowerment center," she adds. "No one should be discounted based on race, ethnicity, gender, religion, age, or sexual orientation. The New Thought Christian is a metaphysician—an explorer of Self and a teacher and student of the laws of Spirit."

## Dr. Harriet Emilie Cady: The Timeless and Timely Metaphysician
(1848–1941)

Harriet Emilie Cady was a woman of her time, and ahead of her time. This relevant, brilliant, and transcendent figure has had a tremendous impact on the development of the New Thought Movement. Additionally her work provides a roadmap and guide into the understanding of metaphysics.

Harriet Emilie Cady was a tremendous spiritual worker, who allowed the "cosmic energy" in the universe to use her to an amazing degree. She and those who were a part of her school of thought were very distrustful of what is termed "the personality." She was more interested in focusing not on the personality or ego of a person but on spiritual qualities. Dr. Cady was invited to teach at Unity Headquarters, a movement she deeply influenced, but she never accepted their invitation. She was a trained physician, and doctor of homeopathic medicine. Additionally, she authored such works as How I Used Truth, Lessons in Truth, and God a Present Help, along with several articles. She, like Charles and Myrtle Fillmore (Unity's co-founders), wrote in a way that was comprehensive and accessible to the reader. Dr. Cady was born in rural upstate New York and returned there for vacations from New York City, where she had a medical practice. Her teacher was the distinguished Emma Curtis Hopkins. "**Nothing is sure at all in your life until it has been put to the test.**" This was this was one of Dr. Hopkins' and Dr. Cady's primary beliefs.

Dr. Hopkins felt that the ultimate aim in life is to come into the consciousness of an "indwelling God." She defined God as "Spirit, the invisible life intelligence underlying all physical things." "God is Spirit and those who worship him must worship in spirit and in Truth" (John 4:24) She further held that God is "An animating or vital principle held to give life to physical organisms."

For Dr. Cady, God is the One Life, One Spirit, and One Power pushing out into various manifestations. God stands under all there is. Additionally, for her God is:

- Substance—Substance means that which is standing under every visible form of life, love, intelligence, or power. ("sub" means under and "stāre" means to stand)
- Power—According to Cady, God does not simply have power. For her God is Power!
- Wisdom and intelligence
- Omniscient—All knowing
- Omnipotent—All powerful

- Omnipresent—God is equally present
- Source of Being—"This Source is the living fountain of all good, the Giver of all good gifts."

## Methodology

1. Have your attention on God as the Source and not on outward appearances. **"Each man must stand alone with his God."** Dr. Cady believed that God is "the spring of all joy, comfort and power."

2. Hold thyself in peace, patience and quietness with the one power and presence in the universe **Psalms 62: 5 "For God alone my soul waits in silence, for my hope is from him."** (Cady) Dr. Cady spoke of an "active passivity" in the silence. Similarly outlined in the work of Dr. Johannes Schultz, professor of neuropsychiatry in Germany, which he termed **"passive concentration"** and **"active concentration."** "Each person must take time daily for quiet and meditation for here lies the Secret to Power." (Cady)

3. Claim your rightful heritage. For Cady "each individual manifestation of God contains the whole; not for a moment meaning that each individual is God in his entirety, so to speak, but that each is God come forth, shall I say? In different quantity or degree" (Cady, p. 8). She further states that Man is the last and highest manifestation of divine energy, the fullest and most complete expression of God. In order for God's Power to work for you, it must work through you.

The continuous speaking of the "word" will bring about the shape or form of supply forth into the visible word. She could penetrate the psychic structure of a person by words and thoughts, which then gave shape to substance.

The Power of Thought is vital in terms of bringing "form" into existence— "There is but one Mind in the entire universe and that Mind is God." For Christian Metaphysicians, Soul is called the "Mortal Mind" (human mind); this is the region of the intellect where we do conscious thinking and there is also free will. The intellect is a servant to the Real Mind. This part of our being is constantly changing. Divine Mind for Cady is the Real Mind. "Let this Mind be in you that was in Christ Jesus" (Phil. 2:5) this Mind makes no errors; it speaks through the still small voice. She encourages us to turn our thoughts away from the external and to the spiritual. This "spiritual thinking" is heightening when we dwell on the goodness of God and the good within each of us. By turning within, you in fact allow Divine Mind or Universal Mind to think through you. The good news is that we have the capacity to change our thinking.

4.  Denials—Denials for Cady is to deny the claims of an "error consciousness," and to declare these claims to be untrue. Denials are a way of spiritualizing the mind and are used to some extent in all traditions and religions. We must remember that the Divine Self is never sick, afraid, or weak. We must deny the suggestions given to us by the carnal mind and embrace the suggestions given to us by Universal or Divine Mind. Denials have an erosive or negation effect.

5.  Affirmations—"To affirm anything is to assert positively, that it is so, even in the face of all contrary evidence." It is a form of training the mind. We should practice denials and affirmations on continuous bases from morning to evening and through the night, until they become a part of our being.

6.  Faith—Cady believed that faith does not depend on physical facts or on the evidence of the senses because it is born of intuition and spirit. "Intuition is the open end, within one's own being, of the invisible channel ever connecting each individual with God" (Cady, p. 65). Faith is the assurance of things hoped for, the conviction of things not seen." "Faith takes hold of the substance of the things hoped for and brings into evidence, or visibility, the things not seen" (Cady, p. 67). According to Cady, desire is very important, for it is God tapping at the door of your heart with infinite supply.

## The ruin of a nation begins in the homes of its people.

*(The Ashanti People)*

Zenovious Sermons Stripling

**Zenovious Sermons-Stripling (1919–1999)**
**Picture of my mother taken from our family photos**

The date of this writing happens to be on Mother's Day. It was deemed fitting on this day to remember my mother and her methods, practices, and service, as it relates to African American women and evangelism. In so doing she becomes a living memorial and I pay homage and respect to the ancestors and make her in the history of African American Spirituality, accessible to the living.

Mother Zenovious Sermons-Stripling was born in Hahira, Georgia, on May 17, 1918. She was the middle child of eleven children born to Elder Johnnie and Mother Eliza June Sermons. Her parents, three brothers, and all of her sisters (four) preceded her in death. She attended public schools in Lowndes County, Georgia.

My mother had a spiritual conversion as a child and, in the words of David, "Your word I have hidden in my heart, that I might not sin against you" (Psalms 119:11 NKJV). She treasured God's word and being endowed with great faith, she always exemplified strength and perseverance in her Christian walk with God. As a young person, she was nurtured and trained in the Church of God in Christ.

She came to Florida as a teenager, first living with her older brother, Amos, and his wife, in Palatka, and then to the city of Jacksonville, where she enjoyed her life for many years. She worked and helped to establish many of the auxiliaries and units in the building of the Church of God in Christ: the prayer and Bible band, "sewing circles, purity classes, the home and foreign mission, sunshine band, missionary circle, and her beloved young women's Christian council. But her work as an evangelist missionary is where she had her greatest impact and influence on the lives of others. She ran revivals in large cities and in remote places (where many would not go), and was a firm believer in the heavenly benefits of prayer and fasting and shut-in ministry.

On April 15, 1942, she married my father, Abner Stripling, who was certainly a leader among men. She was a faithful and loyal wife until his passing in 1982. God blessed their union with five children: Jacqueline, Estella, Norma, Virgil, and me (Phyllis).

Zenovious role as teacher/missionary/evangelist was a position of great importance to her. This "divine appointment," and her commitment and proficiency in it, made her "great" to the people within her sphere of contact. As I reflect on her life, I think of so many spiritually gifted women and men that I have encountered over the years. Many are forgotten by most, and few even remember their names, and most regrettably, their contributions to the advancement of knowledge, culture, and the scared sciences.

This documentation is important for it gives them a place in history, and provides others the opportunity to understand the historical and spiritual evolution of a people. Additionally, a purpose of this work is to provide some of the keys, or certainly links, to the manifestation of advancing knowledge and power in our lives. In this light, we have tools to unlock the door to the spiritual domain. As a result, future generations will understand what allowed our ancestors to survive and thrive during difficult periods of history in this country.

When Zenovious Sermons Stripling spoke, people listened. She was very unorthodox in her methodology. Dramatic, practical, totally engaging, no nonsense, assertive, serious, and not shy in the least. Many during her era, from 1950 to 1980, would say she had "holy boldness" that mixed and mingled with "anointing" (intensified spiritual energy). When observing one of her sessions, you knew you were in the presence of an undeniable, inescapable presence that gave witness to the highest power and force in the universe. Many of her attributes are difficult to put into words, but I must try.

Each generation has it geniuses. The genius in us is the activation of the higher self. My mother could tap into her genius and express it in the "spoken word"—and not just words, but spiritually charged and potent words. Her words went forth with electricity and magnetism that searched out the innermost corners of a person's being and found residence.

Zenovious's sermons were rich with symbolism and straightforward language that was titillating, passionate, stimulating, and exciting. African American Spirituality is just that—exciting. Her word selections were piercing and stunning and contained so much energy that many would go into trance or spiritual possession just listening and receiving her words. It was as if her words became alive and entered us.

Zenovious was a spiritual scientist of sort, a metaphysician of the highest order, a magnificent artist who had the ability to paint a picture of your life with God and your life without God. She meticulously and methodologically took you on a spiritual journey through the portals of "Heaven and Hell" and brought you back by sheer will, unharmed but in search and longing for a "better life." Her ministry as a missionary/evangelist caused a transformation within the individual. She used her voice, her tones, her penetrating eyes, and body movements. "Holistic engagement" would be the term to most adequately describe her methodology. I watched her intently as a child and, as an adult, decided that I wanted some of that "anointing."

As I reflect on some of the characteristics, habits, and behaviors that made my mother great, I would summarize them as follows:

1. She was a firm believer in the existence of an all-powerful supernatural force (God) and believed that this power was accessible to human beings (THE POWER OF FAITH).
2. Her work was activated by an awesome love for God and for her fellow sisters and brothers (THE POWER OF LOVE)
3. She had an incredible memory (i.e., events, scriptures, ideas, concepts and other facts) that would allow one to make connections and draw parallels that would make her positions clear and sound (THE POWER OF CONNECTIVITY).
4. She had a deep knowledge and understanding of the human condition (THE POWER OF KNOWLEDGE).
5. She could disrobe and disarm a person by her logic and conviction, leaving one open to a spiritual transformation (THE POWER OF TRANSFORMATION).
6. She was an excellent storyteller who could bring a story to life, having an interesting beginning that builds to a crescendo and further to a spiritual explosion (THE POWER OF THE WORD).

During and after her sermons people were MOVED: Some cried profusely and became overwhelmed with emotions, some screamed as a release, and others were consumed temporarily by a nonhuman entity or energy, termed the "Holy Ghost" in the Pentecostal experience.

Africans and African Americans, both in the United States and in the diaspora as part and parcel of our cosmology, have embraced and experienced this "ghostlike" entity that could inhabit and consume a person's mind, behavior, thoughts, and body for transformation.

When my mother gave her "messages" (like so many other Black ministers) she became transfixed (someone/something else in addition to her persona), giving her power and knowledge beyond compare. This force was able to channel through her wisdom, spiritual truths, and abilities that far exceeded her eleventh-grade formal education. Her wisdom was as Profound as scholars and academics, along with her delivery style and ability to engage the hearts and minds of others.

An important question for me is, "How did she obtain this power?" Zenovious started every day with a song and prayer early in the morning, while still in bed, in the bathroom, cooking in the kitchen, driving us to school, waiting in the bank or grocery store, or working in the yard. She was constant with a song and prayer. Sometimes a prayer would lead into a song; sometimes a song would lead to a prayer. Sometimes she would combine the song and the prayer. At times, it would be a soft humming, other times the songs were loud and full blown. This depended on where we were at the time, and "the state of the emergency" or need.

The greatest gift my mother gave me was her example and her methodology for awakening the spiritual energy that lies within me and others. However, in many cases it remains dormant. I have chosen to use her practices at times in my own life, and I have found them very effective, along with new models of spiritual transformation I have obtained.

Zenovious passes on to future generations a great and glorious heritage. Her life demonstrated what this book is about, various forms of revelations and manifestations, of which I am proud to share.

Again her methods were based on consistency and focused attention. Her meditative directives along with a strong belief system activated the "God presence" in her life. This formula that I have described is what I believe was central to her profound power as a minister. This, along with her choice to say "yes" to spirit and "yes" to her gift, was part of the spiritual recipe for greatness.

These attitudes, behaviors, and expressions of gratitude, submission, steadfastness, and receptivity were foundational and highly anchoring in great evangelists' ministries. My mother provides one example. I ask myself often if these gifts run in families. I think so, either through nature or nurture or perhaps a combination of the two. It can be passed on by the socialization or enculturation process or maybe it is coded in the genes by the genetic memory of our ancestors. This is a mystery that I don't fully understand.

My mother would say, "It was predestined before the foundation of the earth, so it's God's will." SO BE IT. (ASHE) (AMEN)

THANKS MOM! IT IS FINISHED!

*This Chapter is taken from the book African American Spirituality, Thought and Culture Published by IUniverse.*

# Dream Allies

To assist you into these deep psychological and spiritual realms, I have identified a number of helpers or allies to assist you on your journey, for life is a journey. I would like to caution you before commencing this practice to prepare yourself. This preparation will require a number of things from you.

Prayer and purification are essential. It is believed that one is purified by cleansing one's thoughts and behaviors, by opening one's heart to the power of good, and by faith and by love.

Allies are constructs of your own consciousness. They are self-created aspects of yourself, and are designed to help you establish an ongoing dialogue with yourself to help yourself. Allies are a part of your higher self that are personified and personalized to assist in identifying areas of concern, challenge, and need. These aspects of yourself work under the assumption that no one knows you like you and no one can solve your problems but you and the inner guide in you.

These constructs can be instrumental in helping us funnel or channel these dimensions of self to structure the help we need at any given time. They can help to connect to our divine nature by intentionally isolating and visualizing them. They in essence all point to the source, the power, and the essence. The alpha, the omega, the All. By constructing these constructs you are more conscious of what your needs are and actively seek to discover your needs, your help, and yourself.

By working with these allies, you put the pieces together by ritualizing the process, and as a result you cement and seal them into consciousness as well as value the experience, for you have to participate in your own recovery. Therefore we own it, as we give this process meaning.

By seeing these allies in your dreams you create an avenue to access information. Speak to your allies. Not with your lips but with your mind. Listen to them, and they will provide you with valuable information, to help, heal, and inspire. Your allies will come to your assistance, but you must look for them and ask for them in your dreams.

Remember the overall mission of the allies is to make the message concrete and the interaction more meaningful, and to activate the power within, which many times lies dormant within us. In truth, you have the answer, in truth spirit speaks to you, in truth you are spirit.

## The Priest

The Priest is the anointed one. The priest is on a mission for the good. The Priest sits in an office of great significance. That is the one to bless, and to point you to your power, and to point you to righteousness. The priest will lay hands on you to strengthen and heal. The priest will baptize you with power and holiness and remind you of the great one. The priest will awaken and inspire you and point you to God the Good.

In your dreams, call often for the priest for he has a blessing for you. He will come in his splendor and power. He will help to align and balance you with that power that has no limits.

The priest will enlist you as a soldier in the army of the Lord of your being. The priest is dressed in white and gold. Gold represents the royal priesthood and white represents purity. When evoking the energy of the priest, visualize the energy of white and gold and visualize in your waking hours what your priest looks like. Familiarize yourself with your priest and call on him often, and he will guide you on your path of truth. You will need your priest to help you find your way home.

## The Teacher

Your teacher is another important construct, we all need a teacher. The teacher will instruct and teach you the things you need to know. Your teacher will provide you instructions on how to live ethically, peacefully, and intelligently. Your teacher will show you the pitfalls to avoid. The teacher will prepare you for graduation/coronation into different realms and stages of life.

Use the power of imagination and summon your teacher. See her dressed in yellow standing in front of a blackboard in a classroom. Try to hear what she is saying! Notice what she writes on the blackboard, word, phases, diagrams and illustrations, concepts and theories. What examples does she use? What is the theme or thesis of the lesson she is trying to teach you?

Decode what has been written, discern what is being said, discriminate what concepts are provided. Evoke the color yellow, for it is the color of illumination. Evoke the spirit of your teacher, for you will need her assistance as you are introduced to your various lessons. What is the lesson tonight? What aspects of your self are being taught?

Ask your teacher to explain any part of the lesson
that is still unclear to you and she will.

## The Healer

The healer is the life sustainer, he or she sustains, rejuvenates, and revitalizes. The healer helps to keep your body healed and strong. Call on your medicine man for body rejuvenation. Seek your healer for counsel and for your formula for healing.

Remember to always choose life, and to always choose health when interacting with the healer. Ask the healer to write you a prescription. Remember to ask the healer to identify your healing centers in the body.

Imagine your healer before you wearing the color green. Green is the color representing life, health, and vitality. See yourself and your healer outdoors, surrounded by the sun and water, for sun and water make everything grow.

Tell you healer why you want to be healed, tell your healer why you want to be whole. It is important that you know.

## The Artist

The artist is the creative energy that brings forth beauty and the spectacular into your life. The Creator is beauty! In that vein beauty must be an attribute of the divine. The artist comes to bring more of the goodness into your life. We need beauty and creativity to sustain us, so that our souls can shine. We all need beauty for inspiration, we need beauty for strength, and we need beauty for joy and uplifting, "for the joy of the lord is our strength."

Nature provides a wonderful canvas for the handiwork of the creator. Don't forget to spend time in nature and in the presence of the divine. Your artist will instruct you in the ways of beauty. Your artist will show you magnificent colors, she will draw for you, sing for you, play for you, dance for you. She will recite poetry for you. Your artist will take you to the museum or on a nature walk. Go with her, for she will allow you to experience the beauty to feed and nourish you. As a way to invoke the artist, engage in these activities often.

Ask for your artist on a regular basis; see her in the color orange and she will bless you with her beauty.

I would like to evoke upon you at this time a Navajo Prayer and it simply states:

"May you walk in Beauty"!

## The Psychologist/Therapist

Sometimes we need psychological help! Our therapist's job is to assist us in maintaining psychological balance and equilibrium. Psychologically speaking, we are all neurotic from time to time. These tendencies need to be recognized, addressed, and reconciled. Neurosis is a mild psychological problem that includes our fears, moodiness, drives, impulses, stressors, and feelings of inadequacy, that leave us feeling out of sorts, and out of order.

The psychologist or therapist can lead us to integration, understanding, wholeness, and psychological freedom. The major job of your therapist is to confront and reconcile. The most important level of confrontation is the level of fear. Jesus, a master teacher, constantly admonished us to "fear not." Remember perfect love dissolves all fear.

In your dreams see your therapist wearing a white jacket, for white is also known as a color representing surrender. Our psychological healing is to provide an avenue for distress to leave, for pain to leave, for confusion to leave, for fear to leave. Your therapist will assist you in this process!

## The Friend

We all need a friend to accompany us on this life's journey. Friends share with us, friends listen to us, friends support us, and friends allow us to know that we are not alone. This realization gives us tremendous comfort and strength. Children pick up on this need, and when "real friends" are not available, they invent one. We are allowed to do the same thing. Friends help us out and commune with us. It is important to know that someone has our back, supports us, and cares for us. This realization empowers us to move forward and is essential to our survival. "Friends are the family members we make for ourselves." Solicit their communion in your dreams. Ask them to go with you in areas you feel uncomfortable. Ask them to co/dream with you. It is not uncommon for family and friends to be co/dreamers. This means that they are a part of your dreams, or in some cases have the same dreams.

Invite them to be a part of your dream/soul family. Allow your friends to bless you, allow your friends to help you. Your friends are both male and female.

See your friend/friends wearing the color blue, for blue is a comfort color.

# Dreams and Prophetic Activation

**Lamp in my bed room**

First of all are dreams lawful! According to historical reviews, Dreams have been a source of relevancy and communication throughout cultural traditions and religious and spiritual practices throughout the ages. In the Judeo-Christian tradition, the answer is an emphatic yes!

This is just one scripture in the Hebrew text that makes mention of this phenomena: "In the last days it shall be, says God, That I will pour out my Spirit on all flesh; your sons and your daughters shall prophesy, your young men shall see visions, and your old men shall dream dreams." Acts 2:17

**A brief synopsis of the book Prophetic Activation by John Eckhardt**

(1) Prayer is a key to activate spiritual gifts. Prayer is a means of asking for something, make your request known, it is best to speak out your prayers, because somethings and request are voice

119

activated. It is believed that every word we speak goes somewhere. Words are important and utterance is also. Words have creative power. Words connect you to your subconscious and the comic realm." The Holy Spirit anoint divine utterances. These words carry tremendous power and authority." "Anointed words can bring deliverance, healing, strength, comfort, refreshing, wisdom, and direction. Inspired utterances have a dramatic effect upon men and women. Their lives are enriched through the prophetic words that are spoken. Mere human word could not achieve such results. Inspired utterances are not the work of a man but the Holy Spirit. (Eckhardt, J. p101)

(2) Faith is a primary activator. It has been said that without faith we can do nothing, Faith is the substance of things hoped for, the evidence of things not seen. Faith is a strong belief. Faith launches us into a divine flow and aid in actualizing our potentiality and manifestation

(3) Praise can be a dream and prophetic activator. When you engage in praise and adoration to the highest God, something shifts, and portals open on your behalf, you are open to the flow. When praise go up, blessings come down. "Prophets should be instrumental in worship. They should be involved as musicians, singers, seers, and dancers." "We need prophet-musicians as a part of the worship team. If the members of the worship team are not prophets, they need to be activated in the prophetic anointing. Prophetic people are sensitive to the word of the Lord. The word of the Lord can be spoken or sung" (Eckhardt, J. p112) Many prophetic people especially in the worship experience a "Bubbling Up" where they experience a deep energy and stirring from within, they move, run, speak, clap their hands, play their instruments, and experience an intense move of the Spirit.

(4) Speaking in tongues is one of the ways we edify (build up) ourselves. Prophecy builds up others. The more built up you are, the more you will be able to build up others. We pray in tongues to kick start a prophetic word. Paul wrote: "I desire that you all speak in tongues, but even more that you prophesy." 1Cor 14:5

# Intuition

The Intuition focuses on discerning truth through a direct-albeit unexplained source of knowledge. "The Intuitive suggests that the information sent or received finds its origin inside one's self. (Carlson-Finnerty, K. Gleason, & L. Robinson P.5; **Psychic Intuition**; Alpha Books, 2012)

The Intuition has its origin in the field of Parapsychology, which is a branch of psychology that studies psychic experiences. The term came into use in the 1920s, when the field's founder, J.B. Rhine, created the first institute for psychic research: The Rhine Research Center, situated near Duke University in Durham, North Carolina. (Page 4)

The following exercise is offered to strengthen the intuition and at the same time improve your capacity to be a lucid dreamer, and gain clarity in your dream work.

## Intuition Exercise: Toward Lucid Dreaming

"The first step to learning to control your dreams is to be aware, while you are asleep, that you are in fact dreaming. To do this, start preparing during the day. Pick a common object that might appear in your dreams. You might choose a car, a flower, a cookie, a pair of shoes, a cat, or a tree. Tell yourself several times during the course of your day that when you see your chosen object, it will serve as a signal that you are dreaming, in addition, tell yourself that you will have a lucid dream during the night.

Before you go to sleep, write in your dream journal, seeing a cat (or whatever your object is) will let you know that you are dreaming. Picture your chosen object in your mind and repeat to yourself that the object is a signal. Focus on your breath for a few moments and let the image rest in your mind. When you feel ready, settle down and go to sleep.

When you wake up, write some notes about your experience. Did you see your object in your dreams? Did it remind you that you were in fact dreaming? If not, try again, because practice makes perfect!

If your object did work for you as a signal, try the exercise again. This time, however, in addition to telling yourself about your signaling object, pick a topic to dream about. You might ask your dream to show you which color to paint the bathroom wall. You might ask to be shown your guides. Or you might ask for a fun fantasy experience-why not ask to be shown how to fly?" (Carlson-Finnerty, K. Gleason, & L. Robinson P.124 Psychic Intuition; Alpha Books, 2012)

"Intuition, the direct experience of things as they are. Elephants do it, fleas do it, birds, do it, and bees do it; why should not human beings do it? When we experience the world directly, beyond the filters of conception, we live that world. We are in the world and the world is in us. We can love the world and the world can love us. When we experience only a world preprogrammed by our conceptual conditioning, we merely exist, as if in a dead world. And we destroy all life. The fact that the intellectual authorities of our world have denied intuition for so many generations is a make of imbalance that, if it goes much further, could become mass insanity. No wonder so many people are crying for help. But when the cry comes from the voice of intuition, the only help the medical establishment generally offers is drugs or other methods to dull that voice". (Davis-Floyd and Arvidson, P. Sven, 1997, pix)

Intuition is a type of knowing. It is an insight an awareness that come forth from an unrevealed/ space to the consciousness or awareness. Does intuition come from the cognition or a cosmic and spiritual space? Or questions that are often pondered. Socrates viewed the intuition as a presence, a passion, a voice, an urge that compels one to action.

# Cognition & Mind

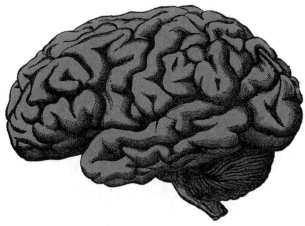

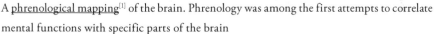

A phrenological mapping[1] of the brain. Phrenology was among the first attempts to correlate mental functions with specific parts of the brain

The **mind** is the set of faculties responsible for mental phenomena. Often the term is also identified with the phenomena themselves.[2][3][4] These faculties include thought, imagination, memory, will and sensation. They are responsible for various mental phenomena, like perception, pain experience, belief, desire, intention and emotion. Various overlapping classifications of mental phenomena have been proposed. Important distinctions group them together according to whether they are *sensory, propositional, intentional, conscious* or *occurrent*. Minds were traditionally understood as substances but it is more common in the contemporary perspective to conceive them as properties or capacities possessed by humans and higher animals. Various competing definitions of the exact nature of the mind or mentality have been proposed. *Epistemic definitions* focus on the privileged epistemic access the subject has to these states. *Consciousness-based approaches* give primacy to the conscious mind and allow unconscious mental phenomena as part of the mind only to the extent that they stand in the right relation to the conscious mind. According to *intentionality-based approaches*, the power to refer to objects and to represent the <u>world</u> is the mark of the mental.

For *behaviorism*, whether an entity has a mind only depends on how it behaves in response to external stimuli while *functionalism* defines mental states in terms of the causal roles they play. Central questions for the study of mind, like whether other entities besides humans have minds or how the relation between body and mind is to be conceived, are strongly influenced by the choice of one's definition.

Mind or mentality is usually contrasted with body, matter or physicality. The issue of the nature of this contrast and specifically the relation between mind and brain is called the <u>mind-body problem</u>.[5] Traditional viewpoints included <u>dualism</u> and <u>idealism</u>, which consider the mind to be non-physical. [5] Modern views often center around <u>physicalism</u> and <u>functionalism</u>, which hold that the mind is roughly identical with the brain or <u>reducible</u> to physical phenomena such as <u>neuronal activity</u>[6][*need quotation to verify*] though dualism and idealism continue to have many supporters. Another question concerns which types of <u>beings</u> are capable of having minds (New Scientist 8 September 2018 p10).[*citation needed*][7] For example, whether mind is exclusive to humans, possessed also by some or all <u>animals</u>, by all <u>living things</u>, whether it is a strictly definable characteristic at all, or whether mind can also be a property of some types of <u>human-made machines</u>.[*citation needed*] Different cultural and religious traditions often use different concepts of mind, resulting in different answers to these questions. Some see mind as a property exclusive to humans whereas others ascribe properties of mind to non-living entities (e.g. <u>panpsychism</u> and <u>animism</u>), to animals and to <u>deities</u>. Some of the earliest recorded speculations linked mind (sometimes described as identical with <u>soul</u> or <u>spirit</u>) to theories concerning both <u>life after death</u>, and <u>cosmological</u> and <u>natural</u> order, for example in the doctrines of <u>Zoroaster</u>, <u>the Buddha</u>, <u>Plato</u>, <u>Aristotle</u>, and other ancient <u>Greek</u>, <u>Indian</u> and, later, <u>Islamic</u> and medieval European philosophers.

Psychologists such as <u>Freud</u> and <u>James</u>, and <u>computer scientists</u> such as <u>Turing</u> developed influential theories about the nature of the mind.

The possibility of nonbiological minds is explored in the field of artificial intelligence, which works closely in relation with cybernetics and information theory to understand the ways in which information processing by non-biological machines is comparable or different to mental phenomena in the human mind.[8] The mind is also sometimes portrayed as the stream of consciousness where sense impressions and mental phenomena are constantly changing.[9][10]

# Memory

An effective dreaming process requires memory at its highest level. Memory of a dream, is especially important for receptivity and synthesis. John Adams once said that "A good memory is needed to get superior performance, whether it is in school, business, or a profession." I would like to add, or in dream analysis, and the working of the subconscious or cosmic mind.

The mind is still active during the dreaming stage. Memory processes figure directly into that state, and are woven into the fabric of dreams. This being the case, it seems reasonable to expect that understanding the psychological nature of dreams, examines the principles by which memories are processed by the mind.

Following trains of thought is important in this analysis. It may be related to words, signs or symbol. Sigmund Freud would draw on themes from the incidents that occurred the following day preceding the dream. Association, in this view, draws on recounting what happened prior to the dream, with the dream. What you are looking for here are connectors in your streams of consciousness. Associative linking, synthesizing and bridging ideas are highly valuable.

Dream images and dream thought are what is needed to be organized, and serves as a major source of thought, memory, and investigation. Emotionally charged conversation, experiences, readings, and events can lend themselves to highly charged and memorable dreams. There are also clues about dream construction, and the utilization of memory in that regard. Memory traces or perceptual residue can bear witness to dream origins and dream analysis. Dream learning, which I believe is also possible, if it is in fact true that the mind is awake in dreaming sleep. A deeper question is how we maintain awareness of awake-ness in our sleep and dreams. For this I believe you need some focal points or memory points. This may require some initial journaling of your day's activities, especially, those activities that were meaningful to you.

Learning and memory involve at least four major processes, according to W. R. Klemm, in his book "Memory Power 101: Registration, Integration, Understanding, and Learning to Learn."

(A) **Registration-** Is the process which detects and encodes data. This stage is deeply facilitated by focus and concentration.

(B) **Integration-** We have a working memory, memory you have just long enough to use it, and stored memory, you can use at any time. In both cases information must be integrated in the working memory.

(C) **Understanding-** Is grasping the concepts, this will allow you to use the information in many ways. Understanding is the bases for greater insights, and creative expression.

(D) **Learning-** To Learn Is the process of learning the rules of learning. This allows for transference to new and different areas of thought, mind, and subject matter.

For Klemm, learning and memory are two sides of the same coin. This learning ability can be generalize to different areas of your life, which is good to know that it is possible to utilized this ability in the dream state. He did not hesitate to say that this can be hard work, like putting a giant puzzle together.

"Memory is stored in the form of enhanced function at the junction points (synapses) between neurons. These synaptic changes occur in the chemical communication systems and in their fine structure. You can say this is the brain's hard drive for memory storage. In simple brains, such as a mollusk's, scientists, can locate where the memory is physically "contained"; But in higher animals, like humans, it is not possible to identify with any great precision where in the brain the memory is. That is because, as one prominent scientist, E. Roy John put it, memory is "not a thing in a place, but a process in a population." (Klemm, P.29)

# Vibration

## Vibrations/Frequencies

Albert Einstein said. "Everything in life is vibration. "Every living thing and matter is made up of vibrational energy. Little is known about how we can use this knowledge to change our lives, and almost nothing is known about how we can use this energy to transform, and enrich our dream state. The question for me is: Does our subconscious, have a force field or is it influenced by vibrational forces as well.

"The thoughts we choose to spend our time on, the ways we react to stressors in our work and our lives in general, the foods we eat, and the substances we use to treat symptoms they all have a measurable, demonstrable effect on our electrical and electromagnetic energies, or 'vibration?' (Openshaw, p.2)

Carefully, chosen music, light, experiences, water, words, people, plant-based foods, methods of worship, meditation, and movements can raise your vibrations.

The choices we make minute by minute affect the kind of day we will have and form the content of dream receptivity.

Everything we eat, drink, see, hear, think, say and dream has a vibration. It is so important to our inner and outer lives that we understand what vibrations are and how to use them to raise our energy.

High Vibe State: love, inner peace, appreciation, gratitude, faith, Low Energy State: Fear, frustration, and anxiety.

"Vibration has its roots in the discoveries of the great Serbian scientist Nikola Teslau During his lifetime, Tesla garnered some three hundred patents worldwide and discovered that absolutely everything has electrical frequency, or vibration energy" Openshaw p.2

There are five basic principles we must understand:

1. Everything is energy, your breath is energy, your toenail is energy, and a shell is energy. Thoughts, words, music, emotions and connectivity to other humans or animals have energy too.

2. You have a Vibration Quotient: When vibrating at a high level you are more likely to do and achieve remarkable and high level things, like get a job, raise, write a book, finish a PhD. Also during this high frequency, you are more likely to fine a high quality mate or high functioning friends.

   When your vibration is high, your cells are multiplying, dividing, and carrying out their purposes perfectly for their full life span until they become obsolete and die a natural cell death-rather than crawling slowly along in the bloodstream, deprived of oxygen, in an acidic medium, dying prematurely or mutating into cancer cells that take over healthy functions.

   When your electrical energy is optimal, you are likely to go out like a light bulb when life is over-rather than fade on the long, painful, slow, dimmer switch of the suffering, low-vibration human (Openshaw pp15, 16)

3. Like Attracts like...it is important to know that you are more likely to attract frequencies that are similar to yours. This is also called the law of attraction. High frequency persons generally seek out frequency and high energy persons, pursuits, opportunities, and ideals

4.  A substance with a Higher Frequency Can Cause the Vibration of a Lower Frequency Substance to increase.

    This has special application to your dreams; you must facilitate the dream life with high frequency people, activities, and thoughts. Reading this book may also help in this regard.

5.  There is an Opposite of the Law of Entropy: This requires that we ascend to higher and higher states of vibrations, Increase what you give to the world and more will be given to you to give.

# The Neuroscience of Enlightenment

In the book <u>Power up Your Brain: The Neuroscience of Enlightenment</u>, David Perlmutter, M.D., FACN Alberto Villoldo, PhD provides fascinating connections between Enlightenment and Neuroscience.

This book looks at Shamanic work, experiences and healing across the globe, these researchers noticed that some forms of meditative or spiritual practices are involved in the radical healing of individuals. These persons tended to use affirmations, prayer, fasting, meditation, in addition to some form of herbs, vitamins and minerals and physical activity or exercise.

They were fascinated with how beliefs, thoughts and emotions have an effect on the body and mind. They provided an explanation of the Prefrontal Cortex and how it could be activated to heal our bodies and minds. These researcher studied societies where people experienced longevity on high levels and found that people tend to live longer lives when:

(A) There caloric intact is reduced
(B) They had healthy relationships (Who they loved and who loved them)
(C) They had ongoing exercise
(D) Avoided or had a minimum amount of meat
(E) Lived with purpose and meaning
(F) Knew how to heal themselves from toxic emotions (forgiveness)

Stress can be a major source of mental and physical illness as well. Acute Stress, which is generally, brief and short lived stress, and Chronic Stress, which is long lasting and highly dangerous. When the body is under long term exposure to stress, stress hormones are released. (Cortisol and Adrenaline)

## BDNF (Brain Derived Neurotropic Factor)

The brain can produce a gene or activate it, which can create new neurons in the brain and can protect existing neurons. These neurons are vital for thinking, creativity, and higher brain functions. This gene can be turn on by:

(A) Intellectual Stimulation
(B) Omega 3 (DHA)
(C) Curcumin- Which can be derived from a spice called turmeric. It is an antioxidant, anti-inflammatory, anti-bacterial and anti-fungal
(D) A lean diet
(E) Exercise- There is a long relationship between exercise and cognitive functioning
(F) Lowering Sugar intake

Researchers believe that by following these patterns, the Nrf2 pathways can be activated and this genetic switch can be turned on,

## The Pineal Gland

The pineal gland also called the third eye is a gland in the vertebrate brain. It is also regarded as a mystery gland and is of great interest to some mystics. For Rene Descartes, he called it the "principle seat of the soul" and the connection between the intellect and the body. This small gland produces serotonin, which is derived from melatonin, a hormone that affects the modulation of wake/sleep patterns. This gland is reddish-gray in color and is the size of a rice grain. Calcium, fluoride, and phosphorus deposits in the pineal gland are associated with aging, meaning that as the brain ages more deposits are collected. The production of the melatonin by the pineal gland is stimulated by darkness and inhibited by light. This gland also plays a major role in sexual development and the calcification of the gland contributes to Alzheimer's disease.

Research done on the psychedelic dimethyltryptamine (DMT) suggests that the pineal gland plays a role in its production in the brain of humans. It is believed that a massive amount of DMT is released prior to death or near death and thus can trigger near death experiences. Many spiritual philosophers suggest the third eye is related to the ajna chakra and also the pineal gland.

Additionally, clairvoyant perception, higher levels of enlightenment and states of consciousness is associated to the pineal gland.

## Docosahexaenoic Acid (DHA)

Perhaps no other brain nutrient is receiving as much attention lately as DHA. Scientist has been aggressively studying the critical brain fat for the past several decades for at least three reasons.

First, more than two-thirds of the dry weight of the human brain is fat, and one quarter of that fat is DHA. From a structural point of view, DHA is an important building block for the membranes that surround brain cells. These membranes include the areas where the one brain cell connects to another, these synapses. This means that DHA is involved in the transmission of information from one neuron to the next and thus is fundamental for efficient brain function.

Second, DHA is one of nature's important regulators of inflammation. Inflammation is responsible for a large number of brain maladies, including Alzheimer's, Parkinson's, attention deficit hyperactivity disorder (ADHD), and multiple sclerosis. DHA naturally reduces the activity of the COX-2 enzyme, which turns on the production of damaging chemical mediators of inflammation. This inhibits the enzyme and helps put out the fire in our brains.

The third and perhaps most compelling reason for studying DHA is its role in modulating gene expression for the production of BDNF. Thus DHA helps to orchestrate the production, synaptic connection, and viability of brain cells while enhancing functionality.

In a recent completed double-blind interventional trial called the Memory Improvement and DHA Study (MlDAS) some members of a group of 485 healthy individuals with an average age of 70 and mild memory problems were given a supplement that contained DHA made from marine algae and some were given a placebo. After six months, not only did blood DHA Study levels double in the group who received the DHA but the effects on brain function, compared with those who received the placebo, were outstanding.

Humans are able to synthesize DHA from a common dietary omega-3 fat, alpha-linolenic acid. But so little DHA is produced by this chemical pathway that many researchers in human nutrition now consider DHA to be an essential fatty acid, meaning that health maintenance requires a dietary source of this key nutrient. Data also show that most Americans typically consume an average of only 60 to 80 milligrams of DHA daily, less than 25% of which researchers consider to be an adequate intake of 200 to 300 milligrams each day.

(Power up your Brain: The Neuroscience of Enlightenment by Dr. David Perlmutter and Dr. Alberto Villoldo, 2011, pages 94 & 95)

# Philosophies, Principles, Laws, Disciplines & Practices

This segment of the book is not on dreams per say, but will be useful in understanding how the universe works. Additionally, it will give us vital tools and disciplines I think are important and needed to facilitate a well-integrated and functional life. As I repeated the statement made by Charles Fillmore in an earlier section of the book "The Universe Operates on Law or it does not"!

I would like to provide at this point, some important terms and definitions as you prepare to read this section of the book:

(1) **Theory-** A way of linking information together in order to explain something.

(2) **Principle-** Is how something works; a principle is also defined as an overall plan.

(3) **Philosophy-** Is the study of general and fundamental questions, such as those about existence, reason, knowledge, values, mind, and language.

(4) **Law-** A System of rules that guide our understanding of how something works.

(5) **Practice-** The observance of religious duties is required of its members. A customary action, habit, or behavior; a manner or routine. Synonyms: custom, habit, pattern, or routine. (Wikipedia)

(6) **Discipline-** Discipline is action or inaction that is <u>regulated</u> to be in accordance (or to achieve accord) with a particular system of <u>governance</u>. Discipline is commonly applied to regulating human

and <u>animal behavior</u> to its society or environment it belongs. In the academic and professional words <u>a discipline</u> is a specific branch of knowledge, learning, or practice. Discipline can be a set of expectations that are required by any governing entity including the self, groups, classes, fields, industries, or <u>societies</u>. (Wikipedia)

## Hermetic Philosophy

Ancient Egyptian Thought is based on Hermetic Philosophy. The Kybalion is a source book of this ancient mystical teaching as expressed by Hermes Trismegistus, called "The Great" and "Master of Masters." Hermes was an Egyptian Master who was a contemporary of Abraham. Egypt is a birthplace of great mystical teaching and hidden wisdom. The Kybalion contains the teachings, spiritual laws, and principles that were outlined by Hermes. In it he teaches the spiritual keys that use and express this sacred mental science.

I.   The Principle of Mentalism
II.  The Principle of Correspondence
III. The Principle of Vibration
IV.  The Principle of Polarity
V.   The Principe of Rhythm
VI.  The Principle of Cause and Effect
VII. The Principle of Gender

## The Principle of Mentalism

This principle holds that we live in and are a part of a Mental Universe. Divine mind is the only essential reality. It upholds, supports, and is first cause of everything that is and shall be manifested or revealed. The "Real World" as we know and don't know it is the expression of "Mind." This "Absolute Power" can be accessed by acknowledgment of this divine power in the universe and understanding the spiritual law from which it operates. The ancient Egyptians called this power "The All."

Mentalism is expressed in creation, creativity, and productivity. It can be called forth through faith, study, practice, and motion. The Word is another building block in the evolution of mentalism. The word becomes life and has its own correspondence. African people and others from the Diaspora are "Word People." This is one major way they express. This is also a way that the divine mind expresses itself from the vibration of words and the meanings they represent. Coming from an oral tradition, the use of this principle was a natural way of tapping into this awesome force. Connecting with "G-d Mind" (Mentalism) is a part of early conditioning and programming that set the stage for the survival and success of this ethnic group and its continual, deeply spiritual essence.

## The Principle of Correspondence

### "As above, so below, so above."
### The Kybalion

The Principle of Correspondence holds that there are many planes and dimensions of mind and existence. The application of this principle is highly useful by understanding the first principle, and that is that we exist in a mental, an organized, and intelligent universe that is lawful and orderly.

This principle or law suggests that we can put into place or into an operation a universe of our making by mixing and matching dimensions by mental imaging, rituals, knowledge, and developing a verbal and mental picture of the world that we desire. We can call this "reality" into being by knowing that there are higher and deeper dimensions, and creating and interacting with them by uniting those worlds through the power of imagination, by looking between the cracks and under the veil to glimpse the sacred, the ALL.

This philosophy was developed by highly evolved creative and spiritual beings. A strong a powerful mind facilitated this ability to be multidimensional. Physical strength is equivalent to mental strength. The root of the correspondence is strength, the mind tells the body what to do and vice versa. The early ancestors were able to connect dimensions and worlds by treating them as one.

## The Principle of Vibration

Nothing is stagnant, all things move, change, and vibrate. The level of vibration is not always constant, however. Human beings can raise or lower their vibration based on what they say, think, believe, and do. An understanding of the fact that everything is in motion, everything is energy, one can begin to connect the dots to spiritual realization.

## The Principle of Polarity

The Principle of Polarity holds that the apparent contradictions, differences, and opposites we experience are simple figments of our imagination. That duality exists only in our minds and not in reality. There is no separation, no paradox, everything is one. Heat and cold, good and bad, light and dark are only degrees of the same thing. We are able to fuse the differences by this understanding and by becoming proficient at making adjustments in the vibrations or in the alteration of the thermostatic conditions.

Chaos theory tells us that seeming contradictions give us the opportunity to create new forms of equilibrium and relationships. Therefore chaos can allow for transformation and harmony. Understanding and using this principle can serve as a great tool for internal and external peace. "We are one." The Jamaican creed is "Out of Many, One" This creed has universal application.

## The Principle of Rhythm

Rhythm is motion that is ordered and measured. The Principle of Rhythm reminds us that the universal operates on rhythm. Consider the rising and the setting of the sun for example. The change of the seasons from winter, spring, summer, and fall. The high and low tides. From this principle you draw inference that one may counter the effects of low times with the realization that with timing and pacing, and waiting, the Cycle of life will turn in your favor. With this understanding, we learn how not to work against ourselves but with ourselves and the universe. This comes largely from paying attention to your life, and by paying attention to nature. The universe has its rhythm, and so do we all.

Early people were masters of rhythm. The drumming, music, and dance are just a few examples of its manifestations.

## The Principle of Cause and Effect

Everything happens according to divine law. Whatever you plant will grow, whatever you reap you sow; if you put something into life, you get an equal or better return. This principle requires like the rest your participation and an understanding of the laws. The principle of causation holds that our thoughts, words, and actions set a form in motion. A favorable outcome follows a favorable input. In their spiritual disciplines this was also the case; serve, pray, fast, worship. The end result was a high level of spiritual mastery. If you put something into it, you will get something out. This is simplistic but at the same time profound and extremely beneficial in building a consciousness for success and spiritual power.

## The Principle of Gender

This principle holds that gender exists on all planes and transcends sexual differences on a physical level. Masculine and feminine energy brings forth birth on all levels of existence: material, intellectual, as well as spiritual. No creation is possible without the interaction of masculine and feminine energy. The logical and the intuitive must harmonize. Theory must meet practice before true progress is made.

This principle teaches to value, affirm, and appreciate both contributions' inputs, and work with both types of forces for the perfection of an idea or practice.

Women were highly valued in many nature-based religions. The priestess, the midwife, the healers, the mothers were highly valued in the community, thus recognizing that the feminine and the masculine forces must work together and be harmonized in order to achieve a complete and workable solution for the needs of the community

The purpose of this section is to assert and identify some of the spiritual principles that have allowed various groups to be strong and assert themselves physically, mentally, and spiritually. Additionally, this work is presented to draw attention to the fact that it was the sacred sciences that were very much a part of many cultures and their retentions that have made a population spiritually potent and undeniable.

## Working with the Law and Principles

**"Fear not little flock, it is your Father's good pleasure to give you the kingdom."** Working with the law or with principles means working with God. Spiritual laws are truth principles. One of the goals of this book is to teach concrete ways to become a master of our circumstances. Everyday application of the spiritual laws is highly practical and empowering. It is important to master your mind and guide it intelligently. It is extremely important to exercise discrimination in all your thinking; it is vital to give your mental life to matters that are absolutely essential; but do not neglect the practical. (Foster, p. 7)

Balance your thoughts to themes of beauty, truth, and progress. Your thoughts make you; your ideals, principles, or ruling desires will determine your destiny. Mental discipline will lead to mind power. Have good and sound reasons for all the views you hold. Form clear and definite ideas regarding your convictions as to why you do as you do and why you think as you think. Mental house cleaning is essential! Deep thinking arouses dormant power, quickens the perception, and leads to the enlargement of the understanding. Psychologists tell us that every individual is controlled by their thoughts. Think good thoughts about yourself and others and the development of your entire being every day. A fatalistic belief is very dangerous. Before an idea can grow, you must be able to see a finished pattern. Every idea must produce after its own kind. Mental photography, like mechanical photography, produces exactly what it sees. (Foster, p. 16)

**The Chapter is taken from the Book African American Spirituality, Thought and Culture**

# Rituals

Rituals are the glue that cements a process or an activity. Rituals are observances, ceremonies, and practices that give validity and sacredness to an activity. Rituals connect one to their beliefs and provide a place and space for ideology and practice to meet. Rituals solidify one's intentionality and provide a public as well as a private opportunity to connect and reconnect one to their spirituality, community, and the self.

Ritual for Somé, in "The Healing Wisdom of Africa" is "the technology that allows the manipulation of subtle invisible energies." (Somé, p. 22) Again, this notion of energy comes to the forefront and the possibility to engage and interact with energy is a recurring theme.

Rituals have the capacity to bring people together. They stimulate the psyche and can provide an emotional catharsis. According to Somé: "There are two parts to ritual: One part is planned: people prepare the space for the ritual and think through the general choreography of the process. The other part of ritual cannot be planned because it is the part that 'Spirit' is in charge of. The unplanned part of ritual is a spontaneous, almost unpredictable interaction with an energy source. It is a response to a call from a nonhuman source to commune with a larger horizon. It is like a journey. Before you get started, you must own the journey. After you start, the journey owns you." (Somé, p. 142)

Rituals for indigenous people are a time for unforeseeable, unplanned, yet orderly disorder. In ritual the soul has the opportunity to express itself fully. (Somé)

"The great advantage of a ritual religious focus is the wholeness that it makes possible. People can feel the forces of ultimate reality, as well as deal with them conceptually. They can dance and sing their way into more than intellectual communion. Ritual alone does not make people holy or mature or mystical, but when people are serious about transforming themselves, becoming realer by closer connection to ultimate reality, ritual offers them a most useful set of disciplines." (Carmody & Carmody, p. 278)

"When most Westerners think of ritual, they are more likely to connect it with words such as empty, old-fashioned, irrelevant, and boring than with words such as transforming, essential, challenging, or healing. Ritual continues to engage the passion and commitment of indigenous people because it stimulates their creativity and their emotions. Most of all, they continue to do ritual because afterward they feel changed. Doing ritual heals people, reconnecting them to the ancestors and to their own deepest purpose. Because ritual is so deeply connected to our humanity to our human nature, anytime it is missing there will be a lack of transformation and healing. If a culture does not draw from ritual, its members will do something else to fill the gap because they have to heal. In the absence of ritual, Westerners turn instead to therapist, self-help groups, or, at a more destructive end of the spectrum, to alcohol and drugs." (Somé, p.146)

When considering ritual from the view point of those from and in indigenous cultures, it is not a dry, formalized procedure, but a transformative process drawing out of the individual the very best procedure for that which hurts, for that which helps, and for that which heals the human spirit. There is a human need to unfold, to actualize, and to synthesize. There is also an essential need to heal, grow, and find the psychological and spiritual balance to continue and proceed in life. Ritual is a healing balm to provide answers or a cure for the soul. Rituals are embedded in symbolism; the psyche cannot be maintained without some feeling of awe, which is found in various symbols that resonate within the individual.

The psyche that is void of this grounding is easily depressed and disillusioned. Finding meaning in life requires focusing the psyche toward a reality that extends beyond the everyday world, and the human psyche requires symbols to maintain that focus. Symbols are important because they point us to a higher and deeper dimension, or consciousness. (Somé)

Mysticism is an ancient art that requires a solid intent, focus, and the ability to channel energy. Because cosmic forces can interact with energy flow, the right conditions are essential. This causes, in many cases, the need for rituals to facilitate the atmosphere and to make the necessary connections to the psyche.

Rituals are the practice, what you do. They have the capacity to lead to a cathartic experience, by allowing for focused attention and an exchange of energy, and as a result they can be transformative. Rituals are the methodologies that connect us to our stories and beliefs (mythology); they cement and solidify the belief by adding a force of fortification. Rituals are a manipulation of divine energy because they are energy in motion. Rituals lift us from the ordinary to the extraordinary. Rituals are a part of a pattern that are extremely necessary for many people around the world to feel connected.

"Why ritual? Because it is through rituals, of many kinds, that we actually work with the various 'levers and switches' that control our experiences of and relationship to the 'world out there.' And it is only as we personally experience that we truly learn the nature and essence of 'the Reality that is,' and evolve in our own portion of that Reality. All mystics, all seers, all prophets, all philosophers, and scientists speak of Universal Truth (or a cohesive system of natural principles), but it is through your own personal experiences that you gain access to the bits and pieces that eventually make up this Truth; Ritual facilitates this." (Sargent, 1994, p. xiii)

Sargent goes on to say that there are various components of rituals: Some are as follows:

1.  Visualization: Before any action or ritual takes place, there must first be some kind of visualization or creative imagination, which for Sargent is period of pre-thinking, or meditation, and is a critical component. Rituals help make the unconscious, conscious

through the process of reflection and contemplation. This aspect is also called psychic centering.

2. Banishing, cleansing, or purification: Banishing means, in a magical sense, the elimination of unwanted thoughts, energies, spirits, spiritual pollution, or bad luck. It is about clearing the ground or providing a suitable launching pad for the energy force to work. It is also about the proper selection of a sacred space. "Some common natural sacred sites are huge caves like Mt. Rainier in the state of Washington, called Tahoma (God) by the Native Americans. Many feel that all sacred sites are or were originally sacred Earth sites, on ley lines (lines of power, or 'nerves,' that crisscross the planet) or located on special power spots determined by gravity, magnetism, or some other expression of natural energy. Whatever reason a place is held sacred, the fact remains that every human culture has holy sites." (Sargent, 1994; p. 7)

## Types of Rituals

Water Rituals "Almost all religious and traditions use water in one way or another as a purifying medium. As Tibetan monks prepare for a puja (ritual or devotion) to Tara or Mahakala, they pour water from a silver vessel, suck it into their mouths and, after swishing it around, spit it out, often with mantra. In Japan, every Shinto shrine has a water trough with sacred emblems on and over it. Before entering the shrine one must take a dipper of the water and wash the fingers of both hands and, as in Tibet, also clean out the mouth before proceeding." (Sargent, pp. 17, 18)

Water rituals have played a major role in religious and cultural rites. Baptism in the Christian mythology is a symbol of purification and revitalization. It also denotes taking on a new spiritual status, being dead and buried to a world of sin, and demarks a new life and relationship being resurrected with Jesus. Baptism has been traditionally symbolic for the washing away of sin and associated with being born again in the Christian tradition. In the Hindu mythology the goddess Ganga represents the Ganges, India's holiest river, and is believed to purify all who bathe there. The god Shiva gave her tributaries so that she would not cause flooding.

"Sacred baths are taken in Brazil, sacred African Rivers, the Ganges River in India, and by Shamans, Priests and adherents all over the world. Why is this bathing ritual so prevalent? We can see it in Africa, Asia, North and South America; in short wherever water is plentiful enough to use for such a purpose! Possibly it is because we are created in the water of the womb. Genetic memory, via the ever-handy group conscious mind, tells us that we came from the primal ocean. We are, of course, over seventy-five percent water ourselves, and the constant need to replenish that personal supply is a key factor in life. Oceans and rivers have also formed the basis of our survival in any number of ways since time immemorial." (Sargent, p. 19, Music Rituals)

## Music Ritual

"All mankind's religions and cultures recognize that song from the heart elevates us to a more sublime emotional and spiritual state. We sing at baptisms, initiations, weddings and funerals: millenary and contemporary melodies, fast and slow, with or without instruments, choral and individual."

Sai Baba "Study music, learn to play, sing, and chant or vibrate at certain notes and in various ways. Plato and Australian aborigines both believe that the music of the heavens is what rules the entire universe, so do the Hindus and a various assortment of other people and creeds. Different instruments invoke different energies as do different kinds of music, tempos of music, styles of music, and so on. Experiment, explore and keep notes."

Sargent (1994; p. 59)

This Chapter is taken from the book Myth, Ritual and Mysticism, by Cognella Press

# Music

Music, like religion, is a power source for many traditions and individuals. Music provides a vibratory or energy sound that adds to our soul life and vitality. The richness of African American music has worldwide notoriety and has given the world fascinating music, including Jazz, which has been proclaimed by Congress as a National Treasure.

Generally speaking, to indigenous people, music is a vital expression of life itself. Music is a form of freedom and release. It allows one to be unbound and free in their emotions and feelings. Emotions such as joy, sorrow, pain, love, hope, and anger are expressed without boundaries or restrictions. For our ancestors music was raw, uncut, unedited, real, and an outflow of the depths of human feelings. This music tells the truth, and causes introspection; it is therapy—it heals you where you hurt. This music has a way a penetrating the innermost core of a person, thereby leaving the feeling of being transformed and transfixed.

Music serves individual as well as group functions. It is highly interactive and participatory in nature, and causes people to be bonded emotionally in a profound and meaningful way. Music has been essential in maintaining group cohesiveness and group continuity.

Music making and performing is a multi-dimensional process. It includes body movements, facial expressions, involves style and dress, is emotionally potent, and declares an internal presence that is inescapable. All of this combines with the music and serves to communicate with its audience and give an overall appeal. During slavery, missionaries had disdain for secular music calling it "Devil's music." For a while these musical abilities were outwardly geared toward sacred music. "The Slave Spirituals" were so powerful one became overwhelmed by their intensity. Also included in the music were secret meanings encoded for meetings and escapes planned. It is believed that the power of the music allowed for a large degree of psychological and spiritual comfort during very dark and difficult days.

African music has its own dynamic, which includes metaphor, instruction, resistance, pedagogy, codes of expression, and generally include an open-ended dialogue. The singer may shout, whistle, yell, or groan, and may present a full range of sounds and behaviors (Hunter). Black music is "So funky" it makes you want to move your body. It appears in many cases that the musician understands how to interact, communicate, and respond to the spirit and human world.

The musician is a talented cultural worker and translator of spirit and envelops a number of qualities and attributes:

- High levels of creativity
- Strong sense of rhythm, timing, and balance
- Discipline
- Dedication to their craft
- Serious in their desire to pursue their endeavor
- Open to be a receptor of creative inspiration

Musicologists tell us that music in general can have positive effects on psychological, physical, and cognitive functioning. Music has amazing effects on the behavior of children, the elderly, those with a variety of mental health needs, and those in pain.

It appears that music for the most part is a human need and human requirement. It is a universal phenomenon that transcends culture and condition that has proven useful in most, if not all, parts of the world.

Music serves the following purposes and provides the following benefits:

- Aids in stress reduction
- Improves communication skills

- Enhances motor skill
- Improves memory and concentration skills
- Elevates self-understanding and self-growth
- Allows for unspoken emotions
- Expresses feelings
- Allows for sublimation or channeling of emotions

## Music Therapy

Trial and error and experience are the best ways to know how music affects you. One approach to implementing your own personal music therapy is by maintaining a music log or journal and keeping a list that includes but is not limited to the following:

- Music that give me a lift.
- Music that helps me when I am physically ill.
- Music that minimizes my stress.
- Music that provides encouragement.
- Music that helps me release my pent-up emotions.
- Music that helps me relax.
- Music that makes me wants to move.
- Music that makes me feels joyous.
- Music that connects me to the divine source.
- Music that facilitates meditation.
- Music that improves concentration.
- Music that heightens romantic emotions.
- Music that minimizes romantic emotions.
- Music that motivates me.
- Music that calms me down.
- Music that aids in pain reduction.
- Music that minimizes depression.
- Music that opens me up emotionally.
- Music that closes me down emotionally.

It would be a great idea to develop a music log. By maintaining a music log, the music that suits your individual needs will be readily available to you in times of need. Additionally, it will assist in minimizing your discomfort and provide the remedy necessary.

Music is a universal gift and privilege—don't neglect the opportunity to heal yourself and make yourself feel better. Music is a proven cure, so let the music play on!

**(This chapter is from the book African American Thought and Culture by IUniverse)**

# Engaging in a Celebration of Discipline

## Celebration of Disciplines

The Spiritual Disciplines are the door to liberation and to spiritual strength. Spiritual Disciplines are not just for Spiritual Giants, but also for everyday people such as husbands, wives, sisters, and brothers, people who have jobs, and people who don't. They are for people who wash dishes and mow lawns and those who care for children as well.

Joy is the keynote of all the disciplines. Laughter is very important; so is singing, dancing, and even celebrating, all of which characterize the disciplines of the spiritual life. The primary requirement is a longing after the divine. Deep calls to deep. Two problems need to be overcome: they are the philosophic and the practical. How do we do it?

One major problem in our society is addiction. Addiction is being devoted to a behavior to such an extent that to attempt to stop the behavior causes mental and physical pain. A fundamental question is how do we handle addiction outwardly? The best approach to dealing with addiction according to Foster, in his book "The Celebration of Discipline" is to touch not, taste not, and handle not. Willpower for Foster is not enough—spiritual disciplines are the answer. They allow us to place ourselves before the creator, so we can be transformed. It is about cultivating our skills and accepting the opportunities given to us. Paramount to this cultivation of discipline is to acknowledge that we need commitment.

Through these various disciplines one can achieve a luscious flow of:

- Love
- Peace
- Patience
- Kindness
- Goodness
- Faithfulness
- Gentleness
- Self-control

It is important to go beyond our everyday activities, for many times they breathe sameness and despair. We must allow our inner guide to be our teacher and our guide. (Foster, 1978)

## The Discipline of Meditation

What is meditation? Meditation is being quiet and still. Meditation is about listening to the divine and reflecting on good words and works. It is also about rehearsing good deeds and ruminating on divine laws.

Meditation allows for the sacred space to listen, become attuned, and to reorganize the self. This space is vital to human growth and development. There are various problems and hindrances to meditation in contemporary society. The major barriers to meditation are noise both inner and outer, hurry, and crowds.

## The Purpose of Meditation

- Creates emotional and psychological space for growth and transformation
- Opens the door to divine mind
- Brings a living reality into our lives
- Allows for inner fellowship

The Goal of Eastern Meditation is to empty the mind and detach. Detachment is "losing personhood" and merging with the Cosmic Mind. There are several misconceptions about meditation. One misconception is that it is too hard.

Christian meditation and Eastern meditation are similar. At the heart of meditation it is about contemplation. Many times contemplation is out of touch with modern life. The Sacred World is available to those who search for it. Meditation allows us to approach the divine for ourselves.

Meditation is also about appealing to the imagination. It is very important to create mind pictures. Additionally we should seek also to purify the imagination though word, thought and deed. (Foster)

In preparation to meditation one should consider: Is there enough time? Are you at peace? Can I find a quiet place? Can I find my center or balance?

## The Forms of Meditation

- Meditate upon Sacred Scriptures
- Meditate upon the Creation
- Give your attention to the created order
- Meditate upon the events of the times and seek to perceive the significance and to gain a prophetic perspective (Foster, pp. 15–32)

## The Discipline of Prayer

Prayer is the most central Spiritual Discipline because it ushers us into perpetual communication with the Divine. To pray is to change and to see things from a divine perspective. A major barrier or problem in praying is a belief that everything is already set. Prayer can transform things. We are working with ourselves to determine the future. Prayer is a responsibility. Prayer may require a learning process. Foster makes the following statements about prayer.

In Prayer, there is no room for the following:

A. Indecisiveness
B. Tentativeness
C. Half-hoping
D. "If it be thy will" prayers

It is vital to pray with expectancy. Let the power of the higher self-flow through you—get in contact with your inner self. In is also vital that one tune in to the proper frequency and listen for guidance.

Find out how the Ultimate Power operates by focusing on the small things first. It is also important that we are motivated and moved with compassion.

- Let love guide and motivate you.
- Pray with openness, honesty, and trust.
- Use your imagination.
- See the situations better.
- See the person healed.
- Envision the relationship restored.
- Imagination leads to Faith.

Don't worry about time. Prayer is a good investment of time and energy, it is worth it. (Foster, pp. 33–46)

## The Discipline of Fasting

Research and books on fasting have been historically very limited. Reason for this disregard of the subject perhaps is the negative reaction to and the bad reputations of Ascetics in the Middle Ages who practiced it.

They gave rise to a very negative perspective of fasting, for the Ascetics were thought to be very excessive.

There is also the propaganda out there that we need three large meals a day.

Many have practiced fasting in and out of Christianity. Some of them are as follows:

- Zoroaster
- Confucius
- Yogis of India
- Plato
- Socrates
- Aristotle
- Hippocrates
- Muslims

In the Bible abstaining from food was generally for spiritual purposes. There are several types of fasting.

They include:

- Normal Fast (Absolute Fast) includes no food or liquid, but water is allowed.
- Partial fast
- Private Fast
- Public Fast

Watching is akin to fasting. This means abstaining from sleep in order to attend to prayer or other spiritual duties. In the strictest sense, Jesus did not command fasting, but discussed it and presented himself as a model and example.

The purpose of fasting: Must forever center on the divine. It is also to ensure the following:

- Enduring power
- Success in prayer
- Spiritual insight
- Healing
- Humility

Fasting can bring breakthroughs in the spiritual realm. Fasting reminds us it is God that sustains us. In a real sense fasting is feasting. An extended fast according to Foster should be ended with fresh fruit and vegetables. (Foster, pp. 47–61)

## The Discipline of Study

We are transformed by the renewal of the mind. Study is a vehicle of thinking, knowledge can be very transformative. What should we study? Study is a movement, a process, and can lead to growth and development.

Study should be orderly and sequential. There are steps in the study process:

- Repetition leads to ingraining habits of thought
- Concentration centers the mind
- Comprehension leads to understanding
- Reflection defines the significance **The Study of Books**
- Is an exacting art
- The need for other supportive books and materials is essential
- It is important to review and discuss what you have read **The Study of Sacred Works**
- It is life transformative
- You need a block of time
- Study away from home

**Some Important Books and Aspects to Study, according to Foster**

- "The Confessions of St Augustine"
- "The Imitation of Christ"
- "The Practice of the Presence of God"
- "The Little Flower of St Francis"
- "Table Talks"
- "The Journal of George Fox" **Study Non-Books**
- Nature
- People

- Culture
- Yourself
- Ask Questions (Foster, pp. 62–76) The Discipline of Simplicity: Simplicity is freedom and it's liberating!

The Christian discipline of simplicity is an inward reality that results in an outward lifestyle. Speech becomes truthful and honest. Having a divine center will meet our needs for security. We need more humane and gentle ways to live.

The bible challenges nearly every economic value in contemporary society.

- Jesus declared war on materialism
- Jesus instructs that "No servant can serve two masters"
- Jesus speaks to the question of economics more than any other single issue.
- It is believed that the Creator does intend that we should have adequate material provisions.

Simplicity is the only thing that sufficiently reorients our lives so that possessions can be genuinely enjoyed without destroying us. We must avoid legalism. The central point for the discipline of simplicity is to seek the kingdom of God and the righteousness of the kingdom.

Jesus made it clear that this approach frees one from anxiety. A joyful unconcern for possessions. We should accept what we have as a gift from the divine. We should also buy things based on their usefulness rather than their status. Reject anything that will produce an addiction in you. Develop the habit of giving things away. Learn to enjoy things without owning them. Be skeptical of "buy now and pay later." Let what you say be simply yes or no. Reject anything that breeds oppression. (Foster, pp. 79–95)

## The Discipline of Solitude

Solitude is vital to our spiritual well-being. Our fear of being alone drives us to noise and crowds. Loneliness is inner emptiness and solitude in inner fulfillment. Solitude is more of a state of mind and heart than it is a place. Great mystics along with Jesus frequently withdrew into solitude. For example:

- After he heard of the death of John the Baptist
- When his ministry changed to a healing ministry
- When calling his disciples
- Before or after any major project

It is believed that human beings need fellowship and solitude. Inner solitude and inner silence work together. The tongue is our most powerful weapon of manipulation. The dark night of the soul, according to St. John of the Cross, allows us to find our divine center. Find a quiet place in and outside of the home. We should discipline ourselves to let our words be fewer and fewer. Try not speaking for a whole day. It is recommended that you should spend time four times each year reorienting yourself. It is also important to keep a journal of what is revealed to you.

Some fruits of solitude are:

- Increased sensitivity and compassion.
- New freedom to be with people.
- New attentiveness to others' needs.
- New responsiveness to their hurts.
- More love and gentleness.
- The opportunity to listen to God. (Foster, pp. 96–109)

## The Discipline of Service

Service is about servanthood. There is a distinction between self-righteousness and true service.

## Self-Righteous Service

- Comes through human effort.

- Is impressed by making impressions.
- Requires external rewards.
- Highly concerned about results.
- Picks and chooses whom to serve.
- Is affected by moods and whims.
- Is temporary.
- Is insensitive.
- Fractures community.

## True Service

- Is unpretentious.
- Cares for the needs of others.
- It draws, binds, heals, and builds.

Humility never seeks gain. It is about virtue. It crucifies the lust of the flesh. Every day should be a day of humility. It produces perfect joy and it endures suffering, hardships, insults, and humiliation for the love of the "All."

Remember service is a way of life. It is about true love and guarding the reputation of others. Service is an act of submission, courtesy, hospitality, listening, bearing one another's sorrow, and sharing the words of life. (Foster, pp. 126–140)

**This chapter was taken from the Book Myth, Ritual, and Mysticism by Cognella Press**

# Benefits of Dreaming

Rabbi Yehuda offers some important insights on Dreams in his book the Dreams Book:

Dreams can be a healing balm. Sleep and dreaming both can help in this regard.

Dreams can provide overnight therapy, spiritually, physically, and psychologically.

Dreams can assist in taking the painful sting out of difficult traumatic and emotional experiences.

Provide for Problem Solving and Creativity. It has also said that we can become smarter in our dreams. The intuition knows more than the intellect.

Dreams can assist in casting off emotionally charged episodes.

Dreams can help in remember details, and provide additional assistance, in terms of integrating information.

As we conclude this manuscript, I thought it was important to review some of the benefits of dreaming.

# Recording Your Dreams

You will need the following equipment:

- A journal or notebook and a pen to keep close to your bedside.
- Another notebook or computer file for listing your own personal interpretations of dream situations or symbols
- A book for reference
- A desire and willingness to dedicate a small amount of time and thought to the dream process

Getting in the habit of recording your dreams is the most difficult part of the process, especially, if you are busy and have to rush off to school or work early in the morning. At least spend a few minutes running the dream over in your mind and record as much as you can remember. Record more details when you have more time.

Write down everything you remember, making diagrams and sketches may help. Try to recall:

- Feelings
- What was going thru your mind as if you were watching a film
- Atmosphere
- Images
- What was the mood of the dream?
- Did anything happen recently to spark this dream? (An argument, or movie before bed)
- Could the dream have been caused or influenced by external things (an alarm, or being in a cold or hot place)
- Is it a recurring dream?
- What do the symbols mean to you personally?

# Conclusion

As I prepared this manuscript. I did so being mindful of for what the nation and the world has experienced. I am fully aware of the issues of the moment, well not fully aware, because our challenges have been so unprecedented and issues we have encountered, so farfetched. I have even wondered: What is Creator up too? I do not want to be like many who have a short memory, and a limited attention span, even though I know, it is a survival strategy to forget.

So, I am recapping a few events, to help us maintain our perspective. To be grateful for what we have done, as individuals, as a nation and world. But, at the same time keep our heads about various individual and global needs and challenges that remain.

A contentious and contested presidential election. Division and hate and wildness! Governmental attempted coups and take overs, fighting, yelling, and cursing in our city streets, in our nation's capital, and all around us. Governmental official's lives and their family's lives threatened and bullied. Political Parties, Family members, former friends, and random people are at odds. Will this become the new normal?

Corvid 19 Pandemic and its aftermath that came in like a flood, killing and hurting our people, and leaving behind a national graveyard, which became so severe that officials did not have enough or a proper space for the dead bodies. The mourning, the grief, the sadness unspeakable. The shuts downs, which left many with no jobs, livelihoods gone, and people do not have money for housing, food, and utilities. Schools closed, children disturbed, and lives disrupted. Education transformed and pressured to fulfill insurmountable needs. Families separated, because travel was not allowed, for periods of time entire airports shut down, global markets shut down, governmental offices shut down.

Mental Health and Mental Stability, threaten, shootings and murders in our larger cities and small towns.

Domestic violence, and abuse off the chart. Depression, anxiety, and full-fledged psychosis among us. Homelessness, Drug, and alcohol abuse still with us.

Ethnic Unrest and Ethnic Pain and turmoil continue to arrest our attention. The scenes of our young people in the country and around the world taking to the streets in protest, and in a pandemic! The murder of George Floyd, and how we watched on television in horror, as his life was being stolen from him, and so many others lives of Black and Brown People. These tragedies have left many wonderings: does Black Lives Matter? Really.

Environmental issues, and global warming pressing, killer storms, unusual weather patterns, fires and water crisis, and animal and marine life in need of attention and resources. However, our focus has been in survival mode.

The War in Ukraine has come upon us, I say upon us, because the world is affected morally, economically, psychologically, and spirituality, by what happens there. Our strategies, and political tools of diplomacy appears inadequate, we have forgotten what is right, what is humane, and seemly cannot find the answers to these problems.

I say all of this to say, we need some strong medicine to endure, we need new and radical approaches, we need new revelations, or action, on the old ones. All of this has also inspired the writing of this book for such a time as this.

Let's keep dreaming until we find the answers we need!

# References

Adeoye Lambo. "Reinventing the Future." Reading, MA: Addison Wesley, 1994.

Ali, A.Y. "The Holy Quran." New Delhi, Goodword Books, 2003.

Angeles, P. "Philosophy." 2nd Edition. New York: The Harpers Collins Dictionary, 1992.

Annas, J. "Plato: A Brief Insight." New York: Sterling, 2005.

Arvidson, P.S. & Davis-Floyd, R. "Intuition: The Inside Story" New York: Routledge, 1997

Asante, M. "Afrocentricity." Trenton, NJ: African New World Press, 1991.

Athey, L. "Latin America." New Jersey: Globe/Modern Curriculum Press, 1987.

Atwater, E. and Duffy, K. "The Psychology of Living." 7th Edition. Upper Saddle River, NJ: Prentice Hall, 2002.

Baker, P "Dreamer's Journey" Coconut Creek, FL, Educa Vision Inc, 2007

Baker, P. Introduction to Myth Ritual and Mysticism, San Diego, Cognella 2013

Baker, P. The Sociology of Religion, Art, and Culture, San Diego, Cognella 2022

Baker, P. "African-American Spirituality, Thought and Culture." Thomson, 2007. ISBN#9780595-44231-7

Baker, P. *Interview with the Reverend Dr. Mary Tumpkin*, Universal Truth Center, Miami Gardens, FL, June 2005.

Baker, P. "The Fundamentals, Principles and Practices of American Spirituality; Kendal and Hunt, 2012

Berg, Y. "The Dream Book: Finding your Way in the Dark: The technology of the Soul, New York, The Kabbalah Center, 2004

"Blaze, C. and Blaze, G. "Power Prayer." Avon, MA: Adams Media, 2004.

Berry, M.F. and Blassingame. "Long Memory: The Black Experience in America." New York: Oxford University Press, 1983. Blackwell, C. and Blackwell, A. "Mythology for Dummies." Indianapolis: Wiley Publishing, Inc., 2002.

Bhaktivedanta, A.C. "Bhagavad Gita as It Is." Los Angeles: The Bhaktivedanta Book Trust, 1972.

Booth, M. Dalichow, I. Healing Through Color, Plant, and Crystal Energy, Carlsbad California, Hay House, 2004

Breshears and Discoll, *Doctrine: What Christians Should Believe*, Reformation 21; 2012, Crossway Publishers, Wheaton, IL.

Broocks, R. "God's not dead" "Nashville, W. Publishing Group,"2013

Brown, D. "The Da Vinci Code." New York: Doubleday, 2009

Campbell, J. "The Power of Myth." New York: Doubleday, 1988. ISBN# 0-385-24773-7 Campbell, J. "Transformations of Myth through Time." New York: Harper and Row, 1990.

Carmody, D, & Carmody, J. *Mysticism: Holiness East and West.* New York: Oxford University Press, 1996.

Carskadon, M.A. "Encyclopedia of Sleep and Dreaming: New York: Macmillan, 1993

Carter, J. "African Religion." *Religion and Culture.* Ed. R. Scupin. NJ: Prentice Hall, 2000.

Castaneda, C. "The Art of Dreaming." New York: Harper Collins, 1993.

Charon, J. & Vigilant, L. The Meaning of Sociology Upper Saddle River, New Jersey Person Prentice Hall, 2009

Colander, D. & Hunt, E. "Introduction to the Study of Society 17th edition: New York Routledge 2019

Conway, D.J. "Maiden, Mother, Crone." St. Paul, MN: Llewellyn Publication, 1994.

Courlander, H. "Haiti Singing." Chapel Hill: University of North Carolina Press, 1939. Crahan, M.C. and F.W. Knight, Eds. "Africa and the Caribbean: The Legacies of a Link." Baltimore: John Hopkins University Press, 1979. Cunard, N. "Negro: An Anthology." New York: Continuum Press, 1996.

Deatsman, C. "Energy for Life: Connect with the Source," St. Paul, MN, Lewellyn World Wide, 2006

Dement, W.C. & Vanghan, C. "The Promise of Sleep" New York, Delacorte, 1999

Dillon, M. "The Handbook of the Sociology of Religion United Kingdom: "Cambridge University Press, 2003

Douglas, R. Decoding Your Dreams, New York, Sterling Publishing Co Inc, 2005

Du Bois, W.E.B. "The Souls of Black Folk." New York: Bantam Books, 1963.

Dunham, K. "The Dances of Haiti." Los Angeles: University of California, 1983. Edson, G. "Shamanism: A Cross-Cultural Study of Beliefs and Practices." North Carolina: McFarland and

Company, Inc., 2009. ISBN# 978-0-7864-3409-1

Eckhardt, J. "Prophetic Activation" Lake Mary, FL, Charisma House, 2016

Ember and Ember. "Anthropology." 8th edition. New Jersey: Prentice Hall, 1996. Encarta Dictionary: English North America. <http://encartadictionary.com>.

Evans. M. "Mind Body Spirit: A Practical Guide to Natural Therapies of Health and Well Being." New York: Anness Publishing, 2000. Feltman, J. Editor. "The Prevention How-To Dictionary of Healing Remedies and Techniques." Emmaus, PA: Rodale Press, 1992.

Fenn, K. "Key Thinkers in the Sociology of Religion." Great Britain, Continuum International Publishing Group, 2009

Fillmore, Charles. *The Revealing Word: A Dictionary of Metaphysical Terms.* Unity Village, MO: Unity Books, 1997.

Finn, Julio. "The Bluesman: The Musical Heritage of Black Men and Women in the Americas." New York: Interlink Books, 1991.

Fontana, D. "The Secret Language of Dreams." San Francisco: Chronicle Books, 1994. Foster, R. "Celebration of Discipline: The Path to Spiritual Growth." New York: Harper, 1978. ISBN# 9780-06-062839-0 Frankl, V. ""Man's Search for Meaning" New York: Washington Square Press, 1984Frazier, E.F. "The Negro Church in America." New York: Schocken Books, 1963.

Freke, T. and P. Gandy, P. *The Complete Guide to World Mysticism.* London: Piatkus Books, 1997.

Freud, S. "The Interpretation of Dreams", New York: Harper Collins Publisher, 1998

Glazer, N. and D.P. Moynihan. "Beyond the Melting Pot." 2nd edition. Cambridge, MA: MIT Press, 1970.

Hall, C.S. "The Sigmund Freud Primer, New York: Harper Collins Publisher, 1999

Hamilton, E. "Mythology." New York: Little, Brown and Company, 1937.

Harner, M. "The Way of the Shaman." New York: Harper Collins, 1990.

Herskovits, M.J. "Myth of the Negro Past." Boston: Beacon Press, 1958. Holliwell, R. "Working with the Law: 11 Truth Principles for Successful Living." Camarillo, CA: DeVorss and Company, 2004. ISBN# 2004108269 Holloway, Joseph E. "Africanisms in American Culture." Bloomington: Indiana Press, 1990. "Holy Bible with the Apocrypha." New Revised Edition. New York: Oxford University Press, 1989.

Hunter, D. "The Lyric Poet: A Blues Continuum." Brooklyn: Caribbean Diaspora Press, 2001.

Hurston, Z.N. "The Sanctified Church." *The Folklore Writings of Zora Neale Hurston.* Berkeley, CA: Turtle Island Foundation, 1981.

Innes, R. "The Book of Dreams: How to Interpret Your Dreams and Harness Their Power" New York, Brown Packaging Books, Ltd, 2000 Isaacson, W. "Einstein: His Life & Universe." New York: Simon & Schuster, 2009.

Johnson, C. "Complete Book of Lucid Dreaming", Woodbury, Minnesota, Llewellyn Publications, 2017

Jung, Carl. "Man and His Symbols." New York: Dell Publishing, 1964.

Jung, Carl "Dreams" Princeton," Princeton University Press, 1974

Kaplan, Max "The Arts: "A Social Perspective. "London and Toronto, Associated University Press, 1990

Kassin, S. "Psychology" New Jersey: Prentice Hall 3rd ed. 2001

Klemm, Memory Power101

Kelly, W.L. "Psychology of the Unconscious. Buffalo, New York, Prometheus Books, 1991

Keesing, F.M. "Cultural Anthropology." New York: Holt, Rinehart and Winston, 1965. Kirk, G.S. "Myth: Its Meaning and Functions in Ancient and Other Cultures." University of California Press, Berkeley and Los Angeles, 1970. (0 52002389)

Kilson, M.L. and R.I. Rotberg. "The African Diaspora Interpretive Essays." *Religions of the Caribbean.* Ed. George Eaton Simpson. Cambridge: Harvard University, 1976.

Kinney, Esi Sylvia. "Africanisms in Music and Dance in the Americas." *Black Life and Culture in the United States*. Ed. Rhonda Goldstein. New York: Thomas Y. Crowell Company, Inc., 1971. Kornblum, W. "Sociology in a Changing World." Florida: Holt, Rinehart and Winston Inc., 1991.

Kottak, C. "Anthropology: Appreciating Human Diversity." 14th Edition, New York: Mc Graw Hill, 2011.

Levin, L.W. "Black Culture and Black Consciousness." New York: Oxford University Press, 1977.

M' Bow, B. *Sacred Vision She Who Possesses the Sacred Eye*. Article published in *The Descent of the Lwa. Journey through Haitian Mythology the Works of Hersa Barjon*. Broward County Library and Kosanba Santa Barbara. December 2004.

M'Bow, B. & Von Lates, A. "Philippe Dodard: Moments Critiques" Galeria Baobab, 2016 Morrison, Dorothy "Everyday Magic." Woodbury, MN: Llewellyn, 1998.

Neimark, P. "The Way of the Orisa." New York: Harper Collins, 1993.

O'Flaherty, W.D. "Other Peoples' Myth." New York: Macmillan, 1988.

Openshaw, Vibrations

Puryear, H. "The Edgar Cayce Primer: Discovering the Path to Self-Transformation." New York: Bantam Books, 1982.

Richards, D.M. "Let the Circle Be Unbroken." New Jersey: The Red Sea Press, 1980.

Segal, R. "Myth: A Very Short Introduction." New York: Oxford Press, 2004. ISBN #13: 978019-280347-4

Saltz, J. "How to be an Artist" "New York" Riverhead Book, 2020

The Art Book: The Big Ideas Simply Explained DK "Contributors Bugler, C, Kramer, A, Weeks, M. Whatley, M, Zaczer," New York", 2020

Sargent, D. "Global Ritualism: Myth and Magic around the World." Woodbury, MN: Llewellyn, 1994.

Somé, M.P. "The Healing Wisdom of Africa." New York: Penguin Putnam, 1998. ISBN#087477939-1 Stata, M. "Nysa: The Life and Words of a Kung Woman." Cambridge, MA: Harvard University Press, 1981.

The Gospel of Thomas 12-14 (The Gnostic Society Library) http:/www.gnosis.org/naghamm/nhlintro.html)

Three Initiates. "The Kaolin: Hermetic Philosophy." Chicago: The Yogi Publishing Society Masonic Temple, 1912. Thornton, J. "Africa and Africans in the Making of the Atlantic World 1400–1800." London: Cambridge University Press, 1998.

Time-Life Books. "The Spirit World." Alexandria, VA, 1992. ISBN 0-8094-9404-3 Vale, N. "The Spiritual Journey of Charles Fillmore: Discovering the Power Within." West Conshohocken, PA: Templeton Foundation Press, 2008.

Van De Castle, R. "Our Dreaming Mind." New York: Ballantine Books, 1994. Villoldo, A. "Courageous Dreaming" Carlsbad, California: Hay House, Inc., 2008

Vollmar, K. "The Little Giant Encyclopedia of Dream Symbols, New York: Sterling Publishing Co., 1997.

Walker, M. "Why We Sleep" New York: Scribner, 2017

Wilkinson, P. "Illustrated Dictionary of Mythology: Heroes, Heroines, Gods, and Goddesses from

Around the World." New York: DK Publishing's, 2007

Wolf, A. "Mind into Matter: A New Alchemy of Science and Spirit." Portsmouth, N.H: Moment Point Press, 2001

Yves-Leloir, J. *The Gospel of Mary Magdalene*. Rochester: Inner Traditions International, 2002.